TIM COUCH

A Passion for the Game

By John McGill and Dave Baker

a **SPORTS**MASTERS book

Sports Publishing Inc.
www.SportsPublishingInc.com

Director of Production: Susan M. McKinney
Editor: Thomas Bast
Cover design: Terry N. Hayden
Proofreader: David Hamburg

ISBN: 1-58382-037-X
Library of Congress Catalog Card Number: 99-65908

A SportsMasters book
a division of
SPORTS PUBLISHING INC.
804 N. Neil
Champaign, IL 61820
www.sportspublishinginc.com

Printed in the United States.

For Bethany and Maddie. Your love fuels my spirit. Your touch calms my soul. You are responsible for my passion. — Dave Baker

For Harold and Aurora, who know a thing or two about awakening to life's possibilities. And for Kris and Buffy, alarm clocks both.—John McGill

CONTENTS

ACKNOWLEDGMENTS

Several people helped to make this book a reality. First and foremost, we'd like to thank Elbert and Janice Couch, who welcomed us into their home and shared their memories, and Greg Couch, whose candor and assistance was invaluable throughout the project. And, of course, to Tim Couch for his role.

Several people at the University of Kentucky were gracious in their assistance and in their openness. We are indebted to athletic director C.M. Newton, coach Hal Mumme, associate athletic director Rena Vicini, director of football operations/recruiting coordinator Claude Bassett, assistant coach Chris Hatcher, media relations director Tony Neely, equipment manager Tom Kalinowski and student manager Jodi Gillespie. Thanks as well to UK players Jeff Snedegar, Dusty Bonner, Quentin McCord, and, in particular, James Whalen, whose insights and wit were as enjoyable as they were quotable.

Several members of the football fraternity were also gracious with their time. We thank University of Mississippi coach David Cutcliffe, Vanderbilt coach Woody Widenhofer, Cincinnati Bengals players Craig Yeast, Artrell Hawkins and Lawrence Wright—and, in particular, former UK coach and ESPN analyst Bill Curry for his considerable contribution.

In no particular order, we also want to thank members of the media, including Tom Leach, Jeff Van Note, Mark Maloney, Larry Vaught, Pat Forde, Billy Reed, John Herndon, Mike Fields, Gary Johnson, John Lewis, Dick Gabriel, and Alan Cutler.

Dave Baker in particular offers thanks to WKYT-TV Vice President and General Manager Wayne Martin, and a special thanks to Steve and Dee Ann Miller and Jim and Jan Brewer for their assistance and never-ending support. "Finally and most importantly, my thanks to John McGill. Were it not for John's call, I would have never gotten involved with this labor of love. And were it not for his patience, I would have been killed in the process. He's a man of great insight and ability."

John McGill in particular thanks Vickie Mitchell, Lorayne Burns, Keith Elkins, Iris Taggart, and Maria Pinczewski-Lee for reviewing some of the chapters and offering valuable suggestions. To Dave Baker, he is indebted for providing critical insights, great humor both on the page and off, extraordinary interviewing skills and writing that enhanced and enriched the Tim Couch story. His efforts were a fine example of the merits of effective collaboration.

—Dave Baker and John McGill,
    September 1, 1999

FOREWORD

Quarterbacks are to me what guitars are to Jimmy Buffett. I've always felt that when it comes to my quarterback, we're going to make some great music together—and have a lot of fun doing it. I suspect ol' Jimbo knows exactly what I'm talking about, even if he can't throw a 20-yard out pattern on third and 19.

Tim Couch can, though.

Can he ever.

When I came to Kentucky in December of 1996 and people didn't know Mumme from mummy—some of them wondering aloud if C.M. Newton had taken leave of his senses in hiring a Division II coach—I looked at films of Tim Couch and knew immediately that if we were going to make some noise, let alone music, this was the instrument to use.

Two years, 8,159 passing yards, 73 touchdown passes, 14 Southeastern Conference and 26 University of Kentucky records later (did I mention seven NCAA records?), the results speak for themselves.

In the earliest stages of building a program at UK, Tim wasn't just the straw that stirred the drink—he was the guy who captivated the state, from Pikeville to Paducah and every place in between. He helped make football fun again. Not to mention successful.

One of the first things that struck me about the state of Kentucky was the amazing loyalty its fans had exhibited through years of disappointment. Then, out of the Eastern Kentucky mountains came Tim, who just as easily could have decked himself out in orange or been a Gator or had his pick of virtually any of college football's cream of the crop. He chose Kentucky—the boldest choice since Julia Roberts picked Lyle Lovett. Some things go beyond conventional wisdom. Some things are a matter of the heart.

Still, you don't win football games with just one player, however brilliant. And you certainly can't build an entire program with one player. However, in terms of being able to jump start what we've set out to accomplish at Kentucky, having a guy like Tim made it possible.

The offense had stagnated pretty good when we first arrived at Kentucky—which is Texan for saying it was pretty non-good. And so had Tim, but not so you'd notice by the time our first spring drills were held in 1997. That very first practice, I knew he was going to be good, and I knew he was going to enjoy doing what we did.

And so it came to pass (what else?) that we got real good, real fast. Having Tim already here when I arrived allowed that to happen, because he could make so many instinctive plays and draw on that remarkable talent of his. If we'd have had to go out and find a guy and recruit him and groom him for a year, we wouldn't have had a chance to be as good as we were in 1997.

We went 5-6 that first year, hardly the stuff of national headlines, but I felt we should have won a couple more games. More to the point, given the overall state of things going into that first year, it was a positive season. We built on that in 1998, going 7-4 in the regular season and earning a New Year's Day bowl bid, Kentucky's first in 47 years. At LSU, we recorded UK's first SEC road win over a ranked opponent in more than 20 years. We were a couple of eyelashes from being 9-2. And when all was said and done, Tim would announce he was leaving for the pros (no surprise here) and become the number-one pick in the NFL draft, by the Cleveland Browns.

There was tragedy, too. All of us, I suspect, learned more in that awful week preceding the Tennessee game than we ever did on the sidelines. A truck crash took the lives of one of our players, Artie Steinmetz, and Tim's closest friend since childhood, Scott Brock—and it ended the college career of Jason Watts, our starting center, whose own life was spared but changed forever. I look back on that horrible time and remember it for all the tears, confusion, anger, sorrow and, yes, compassion.

I also remember it for what I saw in Tim Couch. I saw character and faith. Tim and I talked about prayer a lot that week, and how God has a plan for everyone's life. You second guess everything during dark days like that. You try to make sense of it. And you are left clinging to the belief that every life is important; it's just that some of them are shorter than others.

What's the plan for Tim's life? Well, none of us knows that, of course. But this much I can tell you: There is no player better prepared for the demands of the NFL, no quarterback who brings a more level head or finely honed talent to the game than Tim Couch. He's going to make a lot of coaches look good.

But that's not what separates Tim from the crowd.

What does is passion—a passion for the game.

Let me tell you a little story about that. This happened in 1997, after we had lost at Mississippi State, a game I still think we should have won. By the time we got back to Lexington that Saturday night, it was fairly late. Now, there are NCAA rules about how much time you can spend in the film room, so you never really know if guys are doing all that stuff or not on their own, looking at film and studying to get better.

On Monday afternoon, we're sitting in the film room and I'm pointing out a particular play and Tim says, "Yeah, I saw that." A few more plays go by on the screen, and I point something else out and he says, "Yeah, I saw that." Then I do it again and he says, "Yeah, I saw that." Then I do it again. "Yeah, I saw that."

I look at him and say, "Tim, what do you mean, you *saw* that?"

"Well, Coach," he says, "after we got off the plane the other night, I went out to the TV station and made 'em loan me a copy of the tape, and I watched it all last night."

He'd watched it Saturday night, Sunday morning, Sunday afternoon and Sunday night.

I knew right then we had something special.

And that's what makes Tim Couch extraordinary. He doesn't just embrace football, he breathes it. If the game didn't exist, Tim would invent it. He'd drive up and down the hollers of Hyden, Ky., knocking on doors and getting up enough guys to choose up sides. He'd explain how you play this newfangled game, see, and he'd have them out of their houses and running fly patterns in his front yard. And he'd hit them in the numbers, every time.

A passion for the game.

That's Tim.

And that's music to the ears.

—Hal Mumme, July, 1999

PROLOGUE

In 1989, when the University of Kentucky was searching for a new football coach, a sports columnist for the *Lexington Herald-Leader* made a plea for innovation. Jerry Claiborne had done an admirable job, the only UK coach ever to win five or more games in seven consecutive seasons. But to get to a higher level, the columnist suggested, something more was required.

"The trick at Kentucky," he wrote, "is to keep the other guys guessing—confounding them with short passes, burning them deep when they adjust, and using a running game to exploit things rather than to merely establish ball control."

Seven years later, the columnist was no longer columnizing and Kentucky seemed no closer to innovation in football—even though athletics director C.M. Newton had certainly tried back in '89, wooing no less an offensive genius than current Denver Broncos coach Mike Shanahan, who took a long look before turning down the offer.

Kentucky had gotten a big name coach in Bill Curry, who had become disenchanted at Alabama. Curry was admired as a person but, over time, criticized as a coach—too conservative, most argued, to win with that philosophy. He just didn't have the same talent or depth that the elite of the Southeastern Conference could use to overpower his teams.

That had been the columnist's point all along. If Kentucky was to win consistently, it needed to become the Wee Willie Keeler of the SEC. It needed to hit 'em where they ain't—keeping defenses on their heels with an unpredictable go-for-it offense.

In the fall of 1996, into the drama stepped Tim Couch, the very kind of quarterback—a once-in-a-lifetime kind of quarterback—who appeared fully capable of bringing firepower and talent to a Kentucky offense in desperate need of both.

When Curry was fired effective the end of that season, Newton, who'd certainly made the attempt before, was even more daring in his coaching search. He'd hire an innovative, offensive-minded coach, but he would also hire a no-name.

That Hal Mumme came upon the scene at a time when Tim Couch was around is one of those turning points in Kentucky football history, the ramifications of which may not be fully realized for several more years. Stadium expansion, a higher national profile in recruiting, a surge of fan support ... it all portends greater things.

Even so, it didn't take long under Mumme's system—which indeed focused on short passes, the occasional bomb, and a passing game that set up the run—for Kentucky to explode into of the nation's most powerful offensive teams.

Tim Couch, meanwhile, blossomed into the most watched, most admired and most prolific record-setter in Kentucky football history.

The reformed sports columnist watched all this unfold from a grandstand seat, a "civilian" now. He marveled that a talent like Craig Yeast, who became the leading receiver in Southeastern Conference history, would also just happen to be in place as these exceptional forces converged.

He relished the breakaway magic of Yeast and the cleverness of Mumme's system. But most of all, he watched in awe the talent of Tim Couch, who made the difficult look easy, who fashioned improbable, sometimes seemingly impossible feats so often that they became commonplace.

He remembered what he'd written nearly a decade earlier, how he'd pointed to the model established by Rick Pitino. Pitino had taken over a UK basketball team down in talent after NCAA proba-tion and gotten the most out of it by shooting an absurd number of threes and disrupting an opponent with the fast break and the press.

"Which is precisely what UK football teams have to do," the columnist wrote, "forcing opponents to react to Kentucky's attack instead of just awaiting it."

With Mumme, it was happening. He couldn't have guessed in 1989, of course, that someone as gifted as Tim Couch would be around to trigger it.

In Couch, passion and performance resonated at a level few athletes ever approach.

It was quite a ride, watching Tim Couch lead this revival of Kentucky football.

It was enough to make a reformed sports columnist think that writing a book about it all might not be a bad idea.

Passion will do that for you. —*John McGill*

Kentucky is a most curious state. For years, the Common-wealth has prided itself on being known for fast horses, slow whis-key and pretty women. While most of the world is becoming more interdependent because of things such as the Internet, many Ken-tuckians—especially in the eastern and southeastern parts of the state—are still doing things the old fashioned way.

Each day, thousands of them head off to the mines where coal has been a financial windfall for a precious few. For those who actu-ally go under the ground, it is a terribly difficult way to sustain a meager existence. The toll it extracts is almost always devastating. My own grandfather and an uncle died because of cancer brought on by Black Lung disease—a condition where years of breathing in the coal dust eventually chokes the life right out of its victims. For grandpa, it was a condition developed while he was a foreman at mines in Hazard and Hyden.

Whether it's Hyden in Leslie County or Hazard in Perry County, the people of this region are very much the same. They work hard, are tightly knit and can put up with just about anything—with the exception, that is, of people who bad mouth the Kentucky Wildcats.

In particular, they've followed the basketball teams—ever since Adolph Rupp walked into Lexington and proceeded to make Kentucky the basketball mecca it is today. Walk into a small store almost anywhere in the state, and you're liable to see photos and artwork celebrating the seven NCAA national championships. In Lexington, a state-of-the-art, multi-million dollar museum celebrates nothing but UK basketball. Within the last couple of years, there are two paintings created that capture the essence of what Kentucky basketball means to its citizens.

The first is a scene of men wearing their mining hats, sitting around an old box radio and listening to a Kentucky game. The second is even more telling. It's a painting of a little boy who's fallen asleep on a chair in front of a fireplace on a cold winter's night. Around him are splashes of blue and white, with images of Kentucky and UK everywhere. The title is "Wildcat Dreams," an appropriate rendition of the dream just about every boy in the state has had—to play hoops for Kentucky.

Hyden, Ky., is ground zero for this basketball bedlam. And yet, it is also the home of the state's best known exception—Tim Couch.

Tim Couch played basketball. Played it extremely well—a finalist, in fact, for Kentucky's "Mr. Basketball" award in his senior season. But it was football where Couch truly excelled. And it was Couch who awakened the passion for the game again for Kentuckians—most of whom were too young to recall the days when Paul "Bear" Bryant was the UK coach and success was a given.

Save for a few great seasons in the late 1940s and '50s under Bryant, Kentucky's football program was struggling along in the '90s in much the same way every other UK coach's program had. Blanton Collier was respectable—mostly because he had a 5-2-1 record against Tennessee—as Bryant's successor, but save for a splash of recognition and national ranking under Fran Curci in the 1970s (followed by a cold shower of probation), and a good but not great era under Jerry Claiborne in the 1980s, Kentucky football had mostly been an exercise in futility.

Kentucky fans have always been loyal to the football team. Few if any are the schools with a similar record in the sport that can match the attendance figures UK annually records. Football fervor isn't alien to Kentucky fans. It's just not at the same, near-religious pitch of devotion that basketball prompts.

Until Tim Couch.

Given a passing attack by Hal Mumme that launched his college career, Couch became a finalist for the Heisman Trophy in his junior year. And when he left Kentucky early to play in the NFL, the Cleveland Browns made him the No. 1 draft pick of 1999.

Now, when you stop in a store, you're as likely to see a picture of Tim Couch as you are of the mountain legends of basketball—like Johnny Cox, who led Hazard to a state basketball championship and played on UK's legendary "Fiddlin' Five" that won the NCAA title in 1958; or Richie Farmer, who scored 50 points on none other than Allan Houston in the 1988 state championship game, and who played for "The Unforgettables," the UK team that lost to Duke in what many say is the greatest college basketball game ever played.

Now there is Tim Couch to add to the list of legends. Now there is room for football in the blue-and-white dreams of little boys.—*Dave Baker*

1

The Deuce

If you had to pick one moment—one gem of a moment that captures the essence of Tim Couch—it wouldn't be the pass that found his man in full stride, 40 yards away. It wouldn't be the sprint 50 yards downfield to deliver a block, sending a defensive back head under heels. And it wouldn't be the time—his throwing arm grabbed by an opposing lineman—he shifted the ball to his left hand and squiggled a pass in the flat for yet another completion.

It wouldn't be the pinpoint passes or the raging bull runs or the majesty found in the impromptu artistry of his game.

It would, instead, be the time he was intercepted by Tennessee.

"It was his sophomore year," University of Kentucky tight end James Whalen remembers. "We were walking off the field and Tim had just thrown a 'pick.' When we got to the sidelines, he turned to us and said, 'Boys, I don't care if we lose by one point or a hundred. I'm going to throw every last damn ball I've got, and we're going to play our butts off. We're going to try every last thing we've got to win this game.'"

Passion. It is the essence of Tim Couch's remarkable game.

Couch would throw for 476 yards on that gray day in November, 1997, leading Kentucky to 634 yards in total offense, the most ever yielded by Tennessee in its long, proud and stingy history. Outmanned and over-Manninged (Peyton Manning threw for 523 yards), Kentucky would lose, 59-31. But in defeat, in a season when lowly Kentucky finished a surprising and mostly competitive 5-6, the passion that defines Tim Couch became a passion that surged across an entire state.

It surged from a win over Alabama, Kentucky's first over the Tide in 75 years. It surged from a fake punt on fourth-and-forever against Florida, a fake that succeeded and stamped, once and for all, that this new coach, this Hal Mumme guy, this guy with the hip shades and the even hipper offense, would not take defeat lying down. It surged as Kentucky, 109th in total offense the season before, vaulted to sixth.

Then, in 1998, when Mumme's daring and Couch's command made Kentucky a force no longer to be ignored, the passion was palpable in Commonwealth Stadium itself— where people were finally screaming, yelling and what-the-helling like an honest-to-Bear-Bryant *football* crowd.

Beside the sacred altar of Kentucky hoops, football had found its own lofty niche—not just because winning came more frequently, but because the games themselves were far more competitive and lots more fun. If there's anything worse than losing, it's being boring while you lose. At Kentucky, where the losing and snoozing had become a way of life, football was suddenly alive again. The season was no longer a mere prelude to the opening of basketball practice in October. It even had its own trademark theme: the Air Raid.

There was a Couch in the house and a Jimmy Buffett clone for a coach. It was a dandy pairing. It smacked of promise and pizaaz where only pathos had reigned before, and it ended in a bid to the Outback Bowl. Through it all, Couch shined with a brilliance that may never be matched. In two short seasons in Mumme's system, Couch broke seven NCAA records, 14 Southeastern Conference records and 26 Kentucky records.

Mumme will confirm that it's passion that fuels Couch's game. Bill Curry, the ex-Kentucky coach, will tell you the same—even though it was Curry's clinging to an option offense in 1996 that threatened to squelch the ardor and force Couch, who had chosen UK with his heart, to use his head instead and ponder leaving.

"Most of the qualities that make him unique are not the things that everybody writes about," Mumme says. "Everybody wants to write about his size and his arm and his athleticism, all that stuff. But the thing that makes Tim unique is his passion for the game. He just loves the game. He even loves practice. If he was a guy who didn't get drafted by the NFL and couldn't play football anymore, he'd be out here today, I promise you, throwing the ball around with these guys."

Mumme was speaking from a golf cart during one of his summer football camps for high school kids—a modest undertaking when he first arrived in Kentucky. After UK made it to the Outback Bowl, its first New Year's Day game in nearly half a century, everything changed. Kentucky's long-suffering but loyal fans had filled Commonwealth Stadium year after weary year—but empty seats were popping up with more and more frequency in Curry's final seasons.

All that changed with Mumme and Couch. In the summer of 1999, finishing touches on stadium expansion were increasing capacity to nearly 70,000—and season tickets were already sold out.

"I think you're feeling the effects of the bowl appearance out here right now," Mumme said from his cart. "This time last year we had about 95 in this camp. We've got 220 right now. You need to back it up with more bowls, but we certainly wouldn't have been there without Tim last season, that's for sure."

Mumme would hold five such camps. Two thousand, eight hundred and twelve players would attend. It was not only testament to the coach's growing reputation, it was also a reminder of how Tim Couch had stirred the imagination of young players everywhere. Not to mention coaches. Throughout the state, high schools were taking to the air and loving it. As Mike Fields of the *Lexington Herald-Leader* wrote, the top 20 single-season passing yardage totals in Kentucky high school football have come in the 1990s. In no small measure, the influence comes from Mumme's aerial approach and Couch's aerial fireworks—which had lit up skies as early as 1992, his freshman year in high school when he passed for more than 2,000 yards.

"Tim's passion for football is total," Bill Curry says. "There's some good things about that, and sometimes I think it makes life difficult for him. But having that passion is true of all great champions who get totally focused on their pursuit, whether it's Michelangelo doing a sculpture or Michael Jordan shooting a basketball. Even if he didn't have superior talent, Tim would have been a good player with very little talent because he just loves it so much. The second thing the great ones have is work ethic, and when it comes to football, his is superior. And the third thing he has is magnificent talent. He has great hand-eye coordination."

Passion not only defines him, it drives him. It was there when Couch was a little boy, tossing footballs a hundred times a day at a garbage can in the back yard after school. It was there throughout his high school career, when national records fell and recruiters tripped over each other seeking an audience. It was there at Kentucky, muffled when he was a freshman, then revving up to full throttle in his sophomore and junior years.

And it was there when, in secret, he scribbled down his goals and hid them inside a cardboard box as an eighth-grader.

"It was one of those little boxes like the ones you get when you order checks from the bank," Janice Couch remembers. "Tim got a sheet of paper and wrote on it and put it in the box. He gave it to me and told me not to open it until his senior year. I put it in a drawer—a sock drawer or some drawer with a lot of odds and ends. And I'd forgotten about it until he asked me about it when he was a senior."

When she opened the box, there on the sheet were a number of goals. Among them were to break national records, win a state title and play in the NFL. The state title eluded him, but two out of three, in this case, wasn't bad.

The passion translates into a competitiveness that knows no limits.

Dusty Bonner, the quarterback chosen to succeed Couch at Kentucky, remembers how it surfaced when UK players got up a game of two-hand touch in the summer of 1998.

"We'd play eleven-on-eleven, just having a little fun," Bonner says. "Tim was so competitive. I was, too, and we'd get into it big time. We always put each other on different teams. Well, I ended up throwing a couple of interceptions that day and I was mad. I mean, I was not in a good mood and he was just raggin' me. So we're all going at it, and Tim gets fired up, too. We're getting in each other's face and yelling at each other.

"Well, Tim is trying so hard to make a tackle—in two-handed touch; it doesn't mean a thing—but he hits this guy while trying to stop him, and when he hit him, you just heard a big pop. Tim turned around and said, 'I think my finger's broke.' His finger was just all bunched up the wrong way. He had dislocated his finger playing two-handed touch. Needless to say, that ended our touch football games."

Kentucky linebacker Jeff Snedegar—a former quarterback himself and a nominee for the Butkus Award entering the 1999 season—doesn't trot out the standard attributes when asked what impresses him most about Couch.

"It wouldn't be any of his abilities or anything like that," Snedegar says. "It was just the fact that he could take everything thrown on his shoulders—with the press and attention and everything else—and still be an average person.

"Plus, he's the hardest worker I've ever seen. To be honest with you, I don't think if I was as good as Tim—knowing that I was going to be a first round draft pick and make millions of dollars—I don't think that I could be as dedicated as he was. Don't get me wrong. I ain't lazy, but he just lives and dies football.

"I remember coming out in the fall. We'd be out at six or seven in the morning, and he'd already be out there throwing or running or lifting. Every day I went into the weight room and looked, he was already in there.

"And that's the biggest thing about Tim. Everybody looks at his ability, but they don't know the real Tim. It's just the love he has for the game and the time he puts into it. Everybody thinks he just has all this ability and doesn't have to do anything. It was nothing like that. He was in there twenty-four/seven—working on films, footwork, weights, running, throwing … everything."

Passion and poise were there on the night of August 9, 1999, in Canton, Ohio. In his debut with the Cleveland Browns, Couch hit nine consecutive passes in his first two series during a 20-17 exhibition win over Dallas. One of the throws was a 24-yard, on-the-money rainbow into the end zone. Afterward, he ran like a schoolboy to celebrate with receiver Kevin Johnson—hardly surprising given he was little more than three years out of high school and only through his junior season in college when he opted for the NFL.

Two other plays from that game speak volumes. Taking a huge hit from blitzing Dallas linebacker Dat Nguyen in the first half, Couch quickly got to his feet and showed the same sense of cool command that is his trademark. Then, in the second half with Cleveland having driven inside the Dallas 10, Couch rolled, found nobody open and tucked the ball to cut upfield for the goal line. He lowered his head and collided with several Cowboys. One of them didn't get up immediately. It was Nguyen.

From the pressbox, ABC-TV commentator Boomer Esiason, once a quarterback of note himself and not one prone to gushing, said to his audience: "I tell ya, you've got to love this kid."

"He's a warrior," says Craig Yeast, who was Couch's prime target at Kentucky and became the leading receiver in Southeastern Conference history. "And warriors leave their battle on the battlefield. When Tim went on a football field, that was his battlefield. He left it all out there, every game."

"In high school, Tim's quarterback coach, Freddie Brashear, tried to teach Tim how to slide. If you have big linebackers coming at you, you're supposed to get down, but he wouldn't," says his father, Elbert Couch. "Freddie would just cringe, but Tim never did slide. He never did. I've seen him run over defensive backs where I didn't know if they were going to get up or not. He did it in college, too. I thought he'd killed that guy down at Vandy."

That was in Couch's sophomore season. Vanderbilt, which had an excellent defense despite its lowly status as a team, seemed particularly bent on trying to intimidate and rough up Couch. Once, as he scrambled for a good gain and was pulling up near the sideline when the defense sealed him off, a Vandy player rushed up, seeking to knock him silly. Couch could have simply stepped out of bounds. Instead, he lowered his shoulder and met the player full force. Down went the Vandy player. Couch stood over him, giving him the look—and the look said, "best not try that again."

He was The Deuce when he was a four-year starter in high school, wearing the maroon number 2 jersey for Leslie County High in the remote Eastern Kentucky mountains. He was The Deuce when he played for Kentucky, wearing the blue number 2 that thousands of kids, and a good-sized number of adults, wear replicas of to this day. The Deuce he remains, wearing the No. 2 of the Cleveland Browns after going first overall in the National Football League draft.

"He should be as good as anybody who's ever played football in that league," says Vanderbilt coach Woody Widenhofer, who was defensive coordinator for the Pittsburgh Steelers during the famed "Steel Curtain" era that featured "Mean" Joe Greene.

"It's not the fact that he can make these throws. I've seen him make any kind of throw you can think of," says his brother Greg, another former quarterback. "It's just the situations that he makes them in. He's got composure. I think that's what poise is. You can make these throws when you're just playing around, but when you can do them in a tight situation … I think that's what really separates him." Esiason said the same thing. "What really struck me," he told the TV audience, "was his poise."

Kentucky's sports information department recently compiled "The Tim Couch Quoteboard." It reads like a theater marquee, bright lights flashing. Arkansas athletic director Frank Broyles, who's been around the game in every capacity possible, including a stint as a network color announcer, called Couch "the best quarterback I've seen in 50 years." Louisville coach John L. Smith said Couch was "as good as there is, as good as I've ever seen." Heisman Trophy winner Paul Hornung called him "a John Elway who does

Brett Favre things." Roger Ebert didn't weigh in, but a thumbs up can be safely assumed.

In the unforgiving world of the NFL, such accolades mean little. What matters is surviving, then thriving, in the rarefied atmosphere of uncommon speed, size and talent bearing down on you. What matters is ignoring the criticism that your arm is weak (people in Kentucky are still trying to figure *that* one out) or your foot speed suspect or your ability to lead untested.

Throughout his career, Tim Couch has always put to rest those kind of questions. He did it when some scoffed at the legitimacy of the national record-setting numbers he posted in high school, suggesting he hadn't faced strong enough opposition. He did it again when some said he would suffer at a school with a lower-level SEC heritage like Kentucky, where the talent level around him, they claimed, would not allow him to succeed. Now come the stern jurists of the NFL. Will Couch pass muster? History—and passion—suggest he will.

One reason is because Couch, at a very young age, prepared himself for all of this. That his talent would match his dreams, no one could have guessed. But when his talent matured and became so obvious, Couch did not get lost in the swirl of accolades and media microscopes and questioning critics. He's dreamt this life all along. If he gets to a Super Bowl, he will not be awestruck. He will see it as the natural progression of things.

"Since he was in the fourth or fifth grade he was dreaming about things like that—people coming up and interviewing him and asking for autographs," Greg Couch says. "When those things finally came about—and it started at a young age for him—I think it gradually built up to the point where he was able to take it in a little bit at a time. By the time he was a senior in high school and had all the press coming, it had just gotten to be second nature to him.

"Going into his (professional) rookie year, things aren't going to be smooth all the time. It's going to be rough, and you've just got to fight your way through it. I think he'll be fine. He'll handle it. And I think by the end of year, he'll have composed himself and come out on top."

"The Good Lord made him a good quarterback," Elbert Couch says. "He's been blessed with the skills, but he took it to another level by hard work. I mean, you don't get in the NFL as the number one draft pick by sitting on your butt."

Elbert Couch recently retired from his job as a transportation supervisor for Leslie County public schools. His wife Janice is a supervisor for the State Department of Human Resources. In Hyden, Ky., where everybody knows your name, the parents of Tim Couch live the same life they did before their son became rich and famous. They toyed with the idea of moving to Lexington—which would make for an easier drive to Cleveland and a short commute to Kentucky games. Tim had offered to build them a house there. But Elbert Couch cannot let go of his roots. Hyden is home.

"No, ain't moving nowhere," Elbert says. "You can take the boy out of the country, but you can't take the country out of the boy. I like these mountains. I got friends here. I like Lexington for a day or two."

A while back, Elbert and Janice added on a room to hold all the trophies, plaques and framed photos commemorating their sons' successes. They fill the walls and occupy the floor, suggesting a whole new wing might be in order. Boxes of footballs and shirts and photos sit, waiting for Tim to autograph. "He came home recently and spent an hour and a half just signing things," Elbert says. "He don't have to do that, but he'll do it for kids."

There's an old saying in the hills of Kentucky: *Don't get above your raisin'.* "I always told him," Elbert says, "'Son, don't ever forget where you came from—Hyden, Kentucky.'"

It's unlikely he ever will. There's a twang in Tim Couch's voice that says Hyden. There's a forthrightness in his words that says Hyden. There's the occasional double negative that says Hyden, too—but it rolls off his tongue not as a sour note, but as part of his charm. The wording may be quirky at times, but the intelligence behind it is not.

"He's very bright. When you're good at something, and you know something well, you have no trouble talking about it," says Rena Vicini, Kentucky's assistant athletic director in charge of media relations. "There's no tentativeness or nervousness if you know your subject matter. And Tim knew his, all the time, in dealing with media."

Tim Couch is comfortable when the talk is football and the game is upon him. He was, after all, working at this role at an age when the biggest challenge most kids had was deciding whether to watch MTV or Nickelodeon. If all the focus and preparation have left him a relatively narrow view of the wider world, it's only because football is his world of choice.

He's the Once and Future Deuce, the kid who dreamed it, schemed it and now lives it. It's not just his role, it's his identity. There is plenty of time to expand his horizons, time to grow beyond being just a football marvel. For now, achieving greatness in the game drives him. It is the spark to the passion that never ebbs.

"He's got something about him. He's gifted," Vicini says. "There are some people, like a Rick Pitino, who most believe could do anything he wanted and be successful. I wouldn't say that about Tim, because I can't see Tim separate from football. He's not going to be an entrepreneur."

Not that he'd want to. Not now, anyway. Tim Couch's enterprise is launching a ball that connects with a receiver and confounds an observer over the ease of the act.

"That's all he loves to do, that's all he wants to do, that's all he wants to talk about," his brother Greg says. "He may go fishing every once in awhile or something, but without football, I think Tim would be absolutely lost. If this hadn't worked out for him where he could do it for a living, I don't know what he'd do. He'd probably move back in with mom and dad. That's about all he could do."

As it is, he's doing all he ever wanted to do. His passion has become his profession. How many of us can say the same?

2

No Hidin' in Hyden

Hyden, Kentucky, is no different than most towns in the high hills and low "hollers" of the Eastern Kentucky mountains, where the most influential city planner is Mother Nature. The inclines, valleys, creeks and paths that Daniel Boone once explored retain their character to this day. They dictate how Hyden takes its shape—which is to say, Early American Meander. You don't much reshape or bulldoze through the lay of the land in Hyden. You just follow its lead.

Spread alongside the winding roads and scattered among the narrow valleys are 364 people, one stoplight and more swinging bridges than there are filling stations. There *was* Goofy's Pool Room, where the locals dreamed of one day seeing a Heisman Trophy on display beside the pool cues and pop machine, but the place burned down. And there's coal around Hyden. Lots of coal.

If there's a suburb, it's Thousandsticks, population 30 or so, and boyhood home of Elbert Couch. It computes to right at 33.3 sticks per capita. You could look it up.

UK linebacker Jeff Snedegar, himself a country boy from Salesville, Ohio, took a trip to Hyden once with Tim Couch. They surveyed what the town had to offer. "Tim was like, 'It's small,' " Snedegar says. "I was like, '*Sheeeeit!* At least you've got a Dollar General!' We'd be happy with this back home. You've got to go twenty, thirty miles just to find a grocery store." It's all relative.

Meanwhile, there's the city of Hazard, twenty miles or so up the Daniel Boone Parkway—a toll road consisting of two lanes with the occasional third to let trucks pull over to the right and make their agonized, upward crawls without a train of cars overheating behind them. In the summer of 1999, Bill Clinton came to Hazard. He spoke of the need to inject economic development in the region, and the crowd cheered. He spoke of Tim Couch, and the crowd cheered louder. Bill Clinton knows cheers.

As tempting as it is to say that Tim Couch brought heretofore elusive fame to hidden Leslie County and even more hidden Hyden, the place has tugged at the national consciousness B.C. (Before Couch).

When Richard Nixon finally surfaced publicly after resigning as president following the Watergate scandal, he chose Hyden to make his first speech. The Nixon Recreation Center stands just a punt and a couple of Hail Marys down from one of the Leslie County High School end zones.

Hyden is also where Mary Breckinridge, daughter of a U.S. vice president, opened the Frontier Nursing Service in 1925, bringing the first organized medical care to the region. (Nurses would make their rounds on horseback; as late as 1969, some of them were still using horses.) A few years after the nursing service, she established a school that made

Hyden the nation's birthplace of professional midwifery. In the fall of 1999, the Frontier School of Midwifery would celebrate its sixtieth year. Students come from every part of the nation to connect with the legacy of Mary Breckinridge.

Still, if Couch didn't put Hyden on the map, he certainly was responsible for hundreds of coaches, scouts and national media representatives scurrying to consult theirs. If you throw it, and throw it well, they will come. Throughout the remarkable high school career of Tim Couch, they came in droves.

"I knew everybody in Hyden by their first name," says David Cutcliffe, the head coach at Ole Miss who, as Tennessee's offensive coordinator at the time, led the Vols' extensive recruiting effort. "I had been to the bank, been to the police station, seen everybody's new house that was being built."

And he saw Tim Couch.

"He was a junior by then," Cutcliffe says, "and I couldn't talk to him, but I saw him out there running around and I thought, 'Wow, this is one great looking player.' Mike Whitaker was the coach at Leslie County at the time, and I said to Mike, 'I have not seen one like this before in high school.' It was just evident. He had everything you wanted in a player."

As it turns out, from day one, Tim had all he wanted, too. The first thing Elbert did following Tim's birth on July 31, 1977, was to place a football in his new son's bassinet.

Why did Elbert Couch, lifelong University of Kentucky fan, choose an oblong ball instead of the round one that most people in the state worship?

"Well, I love basketball," Elbert says, "but I've just

always loved football more. I mean, if there was a basketball game in Hazard and a football game in Lexington, I'd go to Lexington and watch football."

What Elbert and Janice Couch couldn't know at the time was just how fitting a choice they'd made. In a few short years, Tim would not only grow to love the game, but would also develop single-minded purpose and singular ability remarkable for one so young. Mozart had his piano. Couch had his pigskin. While the analogy might be a stretch, there is little doubting that Tim was in many respects a prodigy.

Tim's brother Greg, four years older, had talent and determination, too. He would, in fact, wind up playing quarterback for Eastern Kentucky University, leading the Colonels to an Ohio Valley Conference championship and later playing professional ball in Europe. In their formative years, the two brothers would vent their competitive fires on each other.

"We'd fight over who got the last popsicle," Greg says with a chuckle. "Anything that there was to compete at, anything you could think of, we'd do it."

Who'd get the last popsicle? Greg Couch smiles:

"I did. Every time. If we knew we were getting down to the last few, Tim would hide a couple in the back of the freezer. But I'd get one of them and hide it in another spot. When he thought he got the last one he'd come strolling out with it, but then I'd go get the other one. I'd make sure I still had one."

"In grade school, Tim and Greg used to lock each other out of the house all the time," Janice Couch says.

"Once, Tim got so mad trying to get in that he kicked the door and about broke his toe."

Sports, of course, was the natural theater for this competitive war—and war it was. Because Greg was bigger, he always won. Because Tim was so young and wanted to win so much, he would sometimes cry in defeat. Greg would beat up on him for doing so. Then they'd make up, only to resume the battle the next day. In the smallish front yard of the Couch house hard by Rockhouse Road, they'd play football. On the makeshift court that doubled as a driveway beside the house, they'd shoot hoops. Even in the sweltering heat of summer or the dead of winter, they'd play outside for hours on end.

"I've seen them come in and their hands would be so red because it was so cold, but they'd be out there dribbling a basketball," Elbert Couch says. "There'd be seven or eight boys out there playing every afternoon after school."

Sometimes, there'd be just two. Couch versus Couch.

Greg kept winning. But then, one day when Tim was about 12 and was starting to catch up to his older brother physically, a basketball game went down to the wire. Greg rallied, however, hitting the final shot to eke out a win. Frustrated, Tim grabbed the basketball, ran around the side of the house and heaved it in anger.

It crashed through the living room window.

"I didn't see it," Janice Couch says. "I just heard the crash."

Air Raid: The Early Years.

"Eventually I had to take the goal down because it was

costing me too much in windows and doors and every-thing," Elbert Couch says. "Those boys hated to lose."

By the time Greg was a senior at Leslie County in 1991, he was attracting attention. "Greg," his father says, "was a hell of a player." During his tenure as University of Kentucky coach, Jerry Claiborne had expressed strong interest in Greg, who became Leslie County's all-time lead-ing passer. But when Bill Curry took over at UK, the interest waned.

Greg accepted a scholarship offer from 1-AA Eastern Kentucky. As a freshman in 1992 he led the Colonels to the Ohio Valley Conference championship. Most thought that it was the beginning of a great career, but soon Greg was hit with the kind of adversity that, eventually, Tim would also face.

Penn State quarterback John Sacca transferred to Eastern Kentucky and took the job in Greg's sophomore season. Then, as a junior, Greg was supplanted by Tommy Lugenbill, who left Georgia Tech to come to EKU. After a rash of injuries and poor performances, coach Roy Kidd finally went back to Couch as a senior. Although his perfor-mance was more than adequate, Greg had to wonder what might have been. Throughout the ordeal, however, not once did Greg Couch complain, cause dissension or threaten to pack his bags and leave. That's a trait the boys learned from their father.

"There's not been any quit in Greg or Tim," Elbert Couch says. "I always told them, if you want to go out and play sports, or if you want to play in the band, whatever you do you're going to play the season out. You're not going to quit."

That resolve would be tested during Tim's freshman season at Kentucky. But for now, in his formative years in Hyden, there was only the prospect of uncommon talent emerging at an uncommonly young age. Elbert remembers the first time he realized his son might exceed his wildest dreams.

"It was when he was in seventh grade," he says. "Tim was playing on the JV team and we were down to Clay County 7-6, I think, with two minutes to go. We were on our own 10 yard line. Tim threw seven or eight straight completions and beat them 12-7. He threw a touchdown pass on the last play of the game, I believe. And that's when I thought we might have something to take a look at here."

The eyebrow-raising game came in 1990, when Tim, 13, was already 6-foot tall and growing (to 6-3, in fact, by the next year). Growing, too, was the success and interest in Leslie County football. Greg was lighting it up all around Eastern Kentucky. Tim was already his backup. When Greg went off to EKU, Tim stepped in as Leslie County's starting quarterback—as a ninth grader.

Even though the legend was starting to build and some football insiders already had their sights on him, Tim Couch was basically still hidin' in Hyden—still an unknown to most. Because Leslie County is about 130 miles from Lexington and 200 from Louisville, the state's two biggest media centers, relatively few outside the mountains were aware of the remarkable events unfolding. That first season as a high school starter, Couch would pass for more than

2,200 yards. While most of the state and nation remained unaware, mountain residents were taking serious notice.

Football, in fact, soon became The Event in Leslie County. It's probably a good thing the good folks of Hyden never had to pick between a Tim Couch Friday Night Special and a Hank Williams Jr. concert. That would have made the hills alive with the sound of serious cognitive dissonance. (To wit: A pair of road signs herald your arrival into Hyden. One proclaims it the home of Tim Couch; the other is in recognition of the Osborne Brothers, a bluegrass band.) *Are you ready for some foooot-ball!?!* They were, indeed—and most likely they'd have made the hard choice to watch it instead of hearing Hank sing about it.

Before Tim, football in Eastern Kentucky was little more than a diversion until basketball season began. Coaches didn't make recruiting trips into the isolated area, and there was no television station in the region that regularly carried his exploits. There were other players in the past, of course, who'd scored touchdowns and made game-saving tackles, but most didn't go to college. You played ball, you got out of school and you searched for work, hoping for a decent wage—preferably not in the coal mines.

But with Couch—whose talent was so obvious, whose future was so promising—a certain shared dream began to emerge. Many of those former players—grown men now—could see in Couch a symbol that you could make it, that you could reach beyond the area's limited opportunities. In that maroon jersey with the number 2, Tim Couch wasn't just passing a football. He was passing on the heady sense of possibility. With each throw, the implicit message was sent: A country boy can do more than just survive.

It's nothing for thousands to turn out in any Texas town on a Friday night for a high school football game, but for such an event in Kentucky, especially in the mountains, regular sellouts were nothing short of historic.

They were also food fests.

Elbert Couch had started The Quarterback Club while Greg was still in high school, getting together a group of men who became the team's biggest boosters—and eaters. For tailgating, the club chose a prime spot at the top of a hill beside the high school building. Leslie County's football field was in the holler directly below. Just beyond the school, right by the woodworking shop where a decent-sized parking area and a great view of the field loomed, The Quarterback Club found its official home.

At first, the club's membership and menu were modest.

"But it just kept snowballing and snowballing," Elbert says. "We started with a $10 grill we bought at the Dollar Store. Things kept mushrooming to where we had to get a big grill we could pull around in the back of my pickup. It'd fix 50 or 60 steaks and 50 chickens." On Friday nights, it was soon going nonstop.

"I'd take off work a little early on Friday afternoons and get our fixins and get on up to the high school," Elbert says.

Getting there early was paramount. From around the region and sometimes beyond, people began to flock to see the kid throw. If you ventured from Lexington, you drove south on I-75 for 70 miles to London, then southeast on the Daniel Boone for 50 miles until you reached the "Hyden Spur" exit. You drove a few more miles down a winding country road—many times fading into heavy fog trapped by the mountains and trees, wondering if maybe you weren't well on your way into the Twilight Zone, if not oblivion. Cautiously, you'd drive on—recognizing the danger, especially when you saw a car pulled off on the side of the road, one you might have sideswiped had you not been paying close attention.

Then it dawned on you.

It wasn't just one car. It was a whole string of them, lining both sides of the road. Then, through the fog you'd see the glow of the football field's lights, still far away. Somewhere up there a parking lot was already filled. So you pulled off anywhere you could, and walked well over a mile with all the others. You were part of The Event.

"By 4 o'clock in the afternoon, there were already like 500 people up there," Elbert says. "If you wanted on the mountain, you had to park your car up there by 1 or 2—as quick as school let out. If school let out at 3, you'd better already have your butt up on the mountain, because if you didn't, you weren't gonna get no parking place."

Overlooking the field from the club's lofty perch was the province of men. The moms and sisters and girlfriends and children were down in the safe and "traditional" haven of the bleachers, which were filled with people crowded shoulder to shoulder. Up on "The Mountain," the dads got into strategy and play calling. They cursed officials' calls. And they soaked in the view that was, with the crowd and the noise and the lights and traces of fog below, just this side of breathtaking.

In a collective sense, standing there was almost like J.R. Ewing flying over South Fork with bourbon and branch in hand—a smile as big as Texas creasing his face. Truth be told, there *was* some bourbon consumed on that hill—enjoyed away from the judgmental eyes of other adults and the impressionable eyes of the high school kids. More than anything, though, the hill was for people who would never leave Leslie County, who loved it, but who nevertheless saw in Couch the promise of the good life beyond.

Down in the stands there were youngsters who dreamed of being a CEO or a governor or even president. Next to them were twenty-somethings back from their jobs in other cities or even other states, just to see what all the fuss was about. Sitting there, too, were people in their 40s, some who had left the mountains in their younger years, drawn back finally by the down-home values and strong sense of community that is Hyden. This is the place where Freddie Brashear, Leslie County's offensive coordinator, is also president of the local bank.

It was on such a night that Dave Baker, there to file a report for WKYT-TV, got his first glimpse of Tim Couch near the end of his junior season in 1994. Recalls Baker:

I decided to accept an invitation from Jackie Crawford, a Leslie County native and veterinarian who is currently studying to become a doctor. Crawford was also a former UK football player. He had played for Hall of Fame coach Jerry Claiborne, who had come home and tried to resurrect the football fortunes of his alma mater.

Early on in Claiborne's tenure, there were trips to the Hall of Fame (now the All-America) Bowl—but for the most part his teams, while always competitive, were never able to get past the traditional Southeastern Conference powers. Most important, though, Claiborne was hired to clean up the image of Kentucky football, and that he certainly did.

But for thousands like Crawford who live and die with the fortunes of the Blue and White, there was always the longing to beat a perennial power like Alabama or shock the sports world by playing something other than basketball on New Year's Day. Now, finally, Crawford had reason to believe it might be more than just a dream—if Tim Couch would stay in-state and play for the Wildcats.

By inviting me down, Crawford saw a first step in having Kentuckians discover their own "diamond in the rough."

It was a crisp November night and Leslie County was hosting Bell County with a trip to the state football Class 3-A semifinals on the line. The game was being carried live on TV across Eastern Kentucky on WKYT's sister station, WYMT in Hazard. I was going to stop and see the game, interview this young man, and then drive down to Knoxville for our broadcast the next day of Kentucky-Tennessee. I'd planned to later put this high school football story together for Monday afternoon's news telecast.

From the moment I first approached the football field, I knew I was about to see something special.

First was the enticing aroma emanating from the Quarterback Club grill, which hit me from about a mile away. When I finally got to the Club's hillside headquarters, I was struck by the "big time" atmosphere, more akin to college than high school. There were politicians and prominent citizens, bank presidents and the school superintendent—all chewing the fat, literally and figuratively.

It was also my first time to meet Elbert Couch. A man who stands about 6-feet-3, his physique and handshake let you know that this former athlete still had enough strength to deliver a decent block in short yardage situations. Elbert, 47 now, was in reasonably good shape, a result of all those nights refereeing high school basketball. He was also shy but clearly appreciative of the attention his son was receiving.

More than anything, however, Elbert Couch was nervous. He knew the unlimited potential his son possessed. But now, for the first time, people outside of Tim's home turf were taking earnest, studied looks. If that potential was going to be realized, it was the time for "The Deuce" to come up aces.

About 30 minutes before the first snap, I got my first glimpse of Tim Couch. I was simply floored. Here in Kentucky, where thoroughbred racing is a big deal and where each July the most regally bred horses are sold for millions at Keeneland in Lexington, there's something they call "the looks test." That plays as critical a role as anything in the bidding, the record being $13.1 million for a year old, unraced thoroughbred in the early 1980s. In the looks test, Couch was off the charts.

While still a bit thin, he was a big quarterback. Now, lots of high school quarterbacks are tall. Some are tall and even have great arms. Most, though, tend to have the mobility of a 50-year-old man with acute arthritis. Couch was not only big, but athletic as well. Dropping back in the pocket, his feet didn't pound the ground. It was as if his toes were just skimming along the surface.

As for arm strength, not only was he the owner of a cannon, he also had the guidance system to go with it. The kid used to go to the 50-yard line, drop to one knee and bet folks he could hit the crossbar of the goal post. He won more than he lost.

There was also the question of touch. Couch only showed off his arm when he was practicing, like the clip on a UK skills video where you see Couch dropping back and throwing a 40-yard sideline timing pattern that lands in a trash can set up as the target. But he could lay it out there like a feather as well. I never once saw him throw the ball through the hands of a receiver coming out of the backfield because it was too hot. But if you were going over the middle on a curl pattern and didn't have your hands extended, the nose of the football would hit your chest like a drill bit with bad intent.

One other thing impressed me. Here was Tim Couch— who would become the greatest quarterback this state has ever produced, who set national high school records with his passing—also playing defense. No one would have blinked an eye if coach Mike Whitaker (or Joe Beder, who became Tim's coach as a senior) had said, "This young man's too valuable to us on offense to risk playing him on defense." But more than setting records, Couch is about winning—which is why he wanted to play defensive back as well. So there he was, blitzing and sacking, plugging a hole off tackle, intercepting passes in the secondary.

Something else stood out. After the game—a win, as were most games in Couch's career—I decided to get a short interview on camera. A few moments passed, then a few more. I looked over and saw a seemingly endless stream of well-wishers. He talked to them, signed autographs, posed for pictures. "I could be here all night," I thought. So I moved in, extended a hand and introduced myself. I asked if I could get a quick word with him. After all, this was going to be his first real exposure in the major metropolitan areas of the state.

Being a spoiled member of the media, I was sure Couch would immediately drop what he was doing.

"Be glad to," he said, politely enough, "just as soon as I'm finished with these folks."

I was floored—not because I would have to wait, but because of what this kid did next. Every dad, every mom, every boy or girl who came by, Couch took time to make them feel like the most special person who'd come to the game that night.

Better still, you could see that the sentiment was genuine. These were his people. Some didn't have much, but what they did have they spent to watch him. Perhaps more than his incredible ability, this is the reason so many feel a special bond. Even in the mountains, the land of the Hatfields and the McCoys—where distrust and dislike can result from nothing more than being from a different county; where high school sports can often be the most intense example of that separation—Tim Couch was bridging the gap. He wasn't just a symbol for Leslie County. He belonged to everyone in the region.

That sentiment developed early in Tim's high school career. Elbert Couch remembers a game when Tim was still just a freshman.

"We were at Belfry one night," he says, "and after the game I thought there was going to be a fight, because all of these people started coming toward us. But all they wanted was his autograph."

Word spreads when a freshman completes something close to 85 percent of his passes. By the end of his junior year, Couch was a hero to many, and his national reputation was developing. Still, there were doubters—particularly in Kentucky.

As Couch's senior season opened in 1995, Leslie County made its "prime time" debut, playing in the Thoroughbred Bowl in Lexington. There was an odd mix of both excitement and skepticism in the air. People wanted to see these extraordinary skills they'd heard about, but they also wondered if all the numbers and raves hadn't been the result of Couch playing in a safer environment, away from the big schools and big talent, shielded from the allegedly more sophisticated way the game was played. So it was that more than 10,000 people turned up to see Couch and Leslie County take on Class 3-A heavyweight Fort Thomas Highlands, a multiple-time state champion.

Highlands is a 3-A school in terms of enrollment only. With a strong tradition for excellence in football, the school is regarded by many as often fielding the best team in Kentucky, regardless of classification. In fact, in 1998 the two players who finished 1-2 in voting for the state's Mr. Football award—quarterback Jared Lorenzen and tight end Derek Smith, both of whom signed with UK—played for Highlands. The Bluebirds play just across the Ohio river from Cincinnati. Annually, the school goes across the bridge and more than holds its own against the traditional football factories of the Queen City.

The clash with Leslie County was as much cultural as it was athletic. Many people in Fort Thomas identified more with the big city across the river than they did with other parts of Kentucky. If Highlands was "WKRP in Cincinnati," Hyden was "Hee Haw." There was a feeling among the

Highlands faithful that the hip would humiliate the hicks, that the country quarterback had put up big numbers against little or no competition. They were not alone.

They were also wrong.

In what became Couch's coming out party, Leslie County beat the heavily favored Bluebirds 44-42. Couch completed 17 of 30 passes for 287 yards and three touchdowns. But that wasn't all—not by a long shot. He also ran 22 times for 112 yards and three more touchdowns, one of them a 54-yard sprint. But his biggest play was on defense. With Leslie County up 36-35 and Highlands driving late in the game, Couch intercepted a pass at the Leslie County 25 and returned it 32 yards. He then drove his team to what ultimately proved the game-winning touchdown, hitting his good friend Ricky Hensley with a nine-yard touchdown pass.

As Couch told writer Mike Fields of the *Lexington Herald-Leader* afterward: "Northern Kentucky has dominated the mountains forever, so this is the greatest win I've ever had."

From that point on, what Couch did on the field and what he might do in the future was big news. He became the subject of choice around office coffee makers and on radio talk shows throughout Kentucky—and beyond. He would finish his high school career completing 872 of 1,372 passes for 12,104 yards and 133 touchdowns—shattering all-time national records. He would be named the National Prep Player of the Year by *USA Today* and others. No more hidin'—as if he'd ever wanted to. This was his dream, and it was coming true.

Tim Couch came to be viewed as the one player who just might be able to tip the scales, to lift the dark cloud that had regularly visited University of Kentucky football for decades.

But would he come to UK? Would he take up residence in a football graveyard, or whistle on by it?

Elbert Couch thought he knew the answer. But even he wasn't certain.

3

A Farewell to Orange

Outside the Couch home, bitter cold surrounded the darkness and strangled the air. Rockhouse Creek, the small sliver that ran 30 feet or so behind the house, the creek that twice over the years had overflowed its banks and flooded the house, was in no danger of wreaking such havoc on this night. It was frozen over.

Inside, Elbert Couch sat frozen as well—alone in the house, alone with nothing for company but his hopes and his fears.

It was almost 3 a.m. Occasionally, Elbert would hear the wind howling outside—but what he wanted to hear was word of his son's decision. It was the last weekend before Christmas, 1995.

For much of the last two years, life had been a blur—meals taken late at night in the midst of the day's latest batch of recruiting mail. There was never an opportunity to get through the stack without the phone ringing a half dozen or so times. Whether it was coaches or members of the media, "Elbert's Place" was the hottest place in Hyden. Add to that a seemingly endless stream of friends and teammates who'd drop by, at Tim's invitation. But this night was different.

The first real cold snap of winter had hit on this icy, raw night. Instead of the normal abundance of food and drink and conversation, Elbert Couch—who for the last 18 months was always the guy in the middle of the crowd—was now in the middle of his living room, alone.

Out there in the garage—separate from the house, a two-story garage where Elbert had hung on the walls his vast collection of iron skillets and two-man lumbering saws (the ones that Cracker Barrel had offered a handsome sum to use for decoration in their stores)—Tim Couch was alone, too.

Elbert could hear the truck running. Tim had started it up, no doubt, to stay warm as he tried to make a final decision: Tennessee or Kentucky? Big Orange or Big Blue?

It would require a simple response, albeit to a complex question. How many questions and discussions and assessments had they made over the past few years? It seemed endless. And now, the suspense was about to end. Elbert Couch had time to reflect on all that had led to this moment—time to recall what a long, strange trip it had been.

"The first tape I saw of him, he was extremely young. I think he was in the ninth grade," says David Cutcliffe. Now the head coach at Mississippi, Cutcliffe was on the staff at powerhouse Tennessee. He eventually rose to the rank of Phil Fulmer's offensive coordinator, and that meant he was the person who recruited and worked right alongside Peyton Manning. That was an accomplishment itself, but Cutcliffe had his sights set higher. Not only did he get Manning. Now he had a golden opportunity to bring in Couch as Manning's understudy before giving him the ball at one of America's true football factories.

Cutcliffe not only had a great product to offer, he also did a super job of selling it. The recruitment of Couch, however, was unique from that of almost any other high profile player in recent memory. It wasn't a battle between the nation's top five schools, or even a showdown between two programs or two coaches. This wasn't David Cutcliffe going head to head against UK. His opponent was an Eastern Kentucky way of life.

If, as Cutcliffe said, Tim Couch was the best he'd ever seen in high school, was everything you'd ever want in a player, it was likewise true that Cutcliffe was everything you wanted in a recruiter. Still, this was no ordinary challenge—even for one so skilled at wooing supreme talent to Knoxville. Even though comparing UT and UK football at the time was like putting the Chicago Bears next to the Bad News Bears, Cutcliffe knew that in this part of the country he had his work cut out for him.

Because Lexington and Knoxville are almost equidistant from Hyden, Tim Couch's choice of schools was, from the outset, highly likely to be either Kentucky or Tennessee. Like most kids from the mountains, Couch felt a closeness to the region. Like most, he may not have wanted to stay there his entire life, but always the place would tug at you, would call you back. Better to live close enough to get home if you're needed, or come back just to re-charge and regroup.

It's the major reason why Tim Couch did not make the full round of recruiting visits. He popped in at Kentucky, of course, and he and his father drove to Knoxville to watch Tennessee play once—although they left at halftime. The

Floridas and Florida States beckoned, but Couch wasn't interested. Too far away. If any school other than UK and UT had a shot, it was likely Ohio State—since Columbus was about a five hour drive away. But that would be stretching the limits of the geographic comfort zone.

"We never took a single official visit," Elbert says. "We just went to the Bowden Camp before his senior year." That was the big one—a much ballyhooed camp for quarterbacks and receivers run by Florida State's Bobby Bowden and his coaching sons. It was an invitation-only affair, the football equivalent of a black tie extravaganza, restricted to the *creme de la creme* of football. Couch accepted the invitation and walked away with "most valuable player" honors. It served, of course, only to increase the attention he was getting from every corner of the football world.

"It was fun at first," Elbert Couch says.

And how long did that last?

"About a couple of weeks," Elbert says, chuckling. "But then people just started coming to the house all the time. When they weren't here, they were on the phone. We were getting fifty phone calls a day." Meanwhile, a steady stream of rental cars piloted by recruiters began to flow through the hollers and hills. They came to watch, and to pitch.

"We'd see most of the coaches at the game," Elbert says. "They'd come up—Penn State, Georgia, Tennessee, Florida, Alabama, Wake Forest, Ohio State ... all of them." Only three of them reached the sanctity of the Couch home: Kentucky, Tennessee and Ohio State. Actually, there was one other.

"I came home one day and there was Howard Schnellenberger (then coach at Oklahoma), sitting on the couch in there and smoking his pipe, talking to Tim," Elbert says. Give Schnellenberger credit. He'd flea-flickered his way into the house to take his best shot at swaying Couch. Geography and other considerations, though, made it a futile play.

By far the most striking aspect of Couch's recruiting was his shunning the chance to make official visits to campuses. You're allowed five. Few are the kids who pass up the chance to travel and have their egos stroked by grown men anxious to have them play for their school. But Couch pretty much knew what he wanted. Fluff and free rides weren't part of the agenda. According to NCAA rules, high school players can take as many "unofficial" visits as they'd like. Translation: You pay your way and you can be on campus as often as you like. For Couch, that meant a trip to Penn State for a camp, the Bowdens' camp, and that one drive to Knoxville with his dad to watch Tennessee play South Carolina.

"They (the Tennessee folks) were nice, and they've got one heckuva of a program," Elbert says. "They know how to treat you when you go down there, too." But other than the one trip to a Vols game, Tim was in Lexington virtually every time the Cats played when he didn't have a game of his own to play—whether in football or basketball.

Basketball is always a factor when you talk about anything in Kentucky, of course, and Couch was no exception. Despite his unusual football prowess, for a time Couch dreamed of Kentucky hoops as well. He played on Leslie County's varsity from the time he was in the seventh grade. As a junior, he led the state in scoring, averaging 36 points per game.

"I think Tim liked basketball better than football until he was about a sophomore in high school," Greg Couch says. "I know he could have played college basketball. He got a lot of recruiting letters, even after he signed in football with Kentucky. He's just a talented athlete, and an extremely good shooter. I think if that's what he'd put his focus into, he'd have made it to the top."

At a basketball tournament in Columbus, Ohio, no less a figure than Kentucky coach Rick Pitino showed up. He was there to watch Tennessee high school sensation Ron Mercer, but what he witnessed was Couch scoring 60 points. At 6-feet-5, Couch would have been a swing man in college. As a senior, he was one of the finalists for Kentucky's "Mr. Basketball" award.

But by then it was clear that his most promising future was in football. In the end, the decision came down to Cutcliffe and the success of the Tennessee program versus Kentucky—in particular, Kentucky fans. Never underestimate the pull and passion that Kentuckians have for the state school. It vibrates from one end of the state to the other, and it was an extraordinary dynamic that played itself out through Couch's senior season.

Even though it had been four years since the recruiting of Couch took place, David Cutcliffe remembers every detail as if it were yesterday.

"To be honest with you, we probably recruited him harder than Kentucky," he says. "I spent a lot of time. I knew everybody in Hyden by first name. I spent a lot of time with Tim's grandmother. She's retired, but one day she was substitute teaching and I spent half a day in the classroom with her. I taught her class. We were willing to do whatever it took."

It included an unofficial trip to Knoxville in the summer between his junior and senior years—with quarterbacks Manning and Heath Shuler putting the big sell on Couch. Tennessee, which often has the pick of the litter at virtually every position it recruits, was obviously going all out. Kentucky, on the other hand, was acting more like a champion in a prize fight during the late rounds. No hard flailing here. It was as if UK simply wanted to protect a lead.

Nevertheless, the softer sell was spearheaded by one of the most genuine and likable people around—Ray Dorr. The Kentucky assistant had primary responsibility for recruiting Couch, and he'd been around major talent before. At one point he worked with the quarterbacks at the University of Washington, when the roster included Warren Moon

You could see the competitive fire in Dorr, but it was encased in an easygoing personality. On the practice field, Dorr encouraged rather than belittled, taught rather than ordered. He had the gift of being able to sit back and relax, tell a joke, and not make everything in the pressure cooker of college football seem like an epic struggle. When you made friends with Ray Dorr, you made a friend for life. He gave that cliché meaning, and his down home sincerity played well with the Couches—especially with Tim.

Dave Baker recalls:

I remember the last practice that Bill Curry and his staff conducted at Kentucky in 1996. It was a cold November Thursday. The days were getting shorter, and by the time practice had ended, dusk had begun to fall. It was symbolic—

a gray pall over what had been an excruciating season for everyone involved.

With Curry already fired and their jobs about to end, many of the coaches felt they had gotten a raw deal—or no longer felt a sense of responsibility. When practice ended, instead of coming off the field the way they'd always done to file past a handful of reporters, they scurried to the far end of the stadium and retreated to the locked doors of their offices.

There was one exception. Still out there at mid-field was a quarterback whose name I can't even recall. He had to be fourth or fifth on the depth chart. He had no chance of getting into Saturday's game. But there he was, still working, still trying to improve. His position coach was out there, too, displaying the kind of positive spirit you'd normally see on the first morning of two-a-days. It was Dorr. And it's an image that has never escaped me. Ray Dorr is an assistant at Texas A&M now, even though he's been diagnosed with Lou Gehrig's disease. That puts the gloom of that November day in perspective, but what Dorr did that day is what he does now in facing his disease—still full of enthusiasm, still a believer in hope. It was something Tim Couch saw in him as well, and it played a significant role in Tim's decision.

If Dorr had been the offensive coordinator at Kentucky, this recruiting battle might have been over long before. But the man who held that title was Elliot Uzelac—more remote, and certainly more conservative when it came to offensive strategy. Bill Curry saw the role of a head coach as "chairman of the board." Each day he would survey practice from an observation tower placed between two practice fields. In order to be successful with that approach, you've got to have strong coordinators on both sides of the ball.

The year before, Curry found that success by bringing in Mike Archer to coordinate the defense. A former head coach at LSU and now the linebackers coach of the Pittsburgh Steelers, Archer put the bite back in Kentucky's defense. Curry, believing the offense needed the same sort of toughness and attitude, brought in Uzelac, who had a reputation for rump kicking. It was not a quality that always served him well. A few years earlier, Uzelac was the man in the center of a very public spat with Ohio State running back Robert Smith. Smith alleged that Uzelac wanted him to spend less time in class and more time on the football field. That led to Smith leaving. In a storm of controversy, Uzelac then left Ohio State and Smith returned.

Uzelac went to Colorado, where he was a part of the Buffaloes' resurgence under Bill McCartney. When McCartney suddenly retired to run a men's religious movement known as Promise Keepers, a young Rick Neuheisel got the job. The ex-UCLA quarterback wanted Uzelac to stay on as coordinator, but only if he dropped the option portion of his package. As you may have guessed by now, Uzelac and compromise are not two words used in conjunction with one another very often. So he applied and got the job on Curry's staff.

He came to Central Kentucky and found quarterbacks that weren't pure drop back passers, making the transition to his option offense quite easy. It was that offense—and the question of whether this "old dog" could truly learn a new offensive trick—that kept Tennessee in the Couch recruiting game.

Publicly and privately, you never got the sense that to the UK staff Couch was a make-or-break recruit. Tennessee was just the opposite, and that's why Cutcliffe kept the hammer down. In the end, the deciding factor was quality of life. Tennessee was offering Couch a chance to get out of the mountains and step into the kind of high-profile program most athletes dream of.

Tim Couch, however, was wrestling with his own passion. Couldn't he do the same things at Kentucky? Couldn't he help get the UK program back into the bowl picture and at the same time catch the eyes of the NFL scouts? Wouldn't it be better to help bring prominence to the program that his father had followed so earnestly all these decades? It was a dice roll that was debated publicly and privately by people across Kentucky and Tennessee. It was also debated by Couch the entire fall of 1995.

It became tougher and tougher to declare a winner. Kentucky's offense continued to sputter along, but that negative seemed to be canceled out by the success of Peyton Manning, only a sophomore and firmly ensconced as the Vols' quarterback. While Manning was indeed playing well, there was no guarantee that he might head to the pros early. (And he didn't, staying with Tennessee through the 1997 season).

Among all the principals in the recruiting of Couch, nothing was taken for granted. Through Couch's junior year, Mike Whitaker was his head coach. Whitaker had been a standout in his own right at Leslie County, and then played for Kentucky. But things didn't click with Jerry Claiborne and his staff, and Whitaker transferred to Eastern Kentucky. Because of that, some close to the Leslie County football scene fretted that Whitaker might be encouraging Tim to go to Tennessee. There are those who suspect that it was the reason Whitaker was gone and Joe Beder was Couch's coach for his senior season.

As decision day grew nearer, some were convinced that the 1995 Kentucky-Tennessee game might be the final determining factor in Couch's decision. If the Vols could roll up a big win, the conventional wisdom in Knoxville went, Couch would come to the conclusion that the UK situation was hopeless. If true, that part of the equation fell on its face. Although Tennessee was a huge favorite, Kentucky played a tremendous game. The Vols had to rally to escape with a 34-31 win.

At halftime of that game, Kentucky athletics director C.M. Newton made his contribution to the recruiting process.

"I met with Tim because the coaches asked me to," Newton says. "And I told him the Leon Douglas story. (Douglas was the first major recruit that Newton got to stay in state when he was basketball coach at Alabama). I told him how critical it was to this university. And I said, 'You could be a real difference-maker, but that's not the reason you should come here. You've got to decide on those reasons yourself. But I just want you to know from our standpoint, everybody *wants* you, but there might be one place that *needs* you. And put that into your equation.' And I really believe that. Tennessee didn't need him. They wanted him. We not only wanted, we needed. That's what got *me* back here. Other people had wanted me, but the fact that they convinced me I was needed … and so I talked to him about that."

You could plan for weeks and months and not hit Tim Couch with a more effective recruiting pitch. Newton's words carried a weight that struck at the crux of the matter. Couch knew how Kentucky fans yearned to see him forsake the big-name football schools and bring them something to cheer about. But to hear it from Newton, and to hear it from someone who himself became UK's athletics director with a decision made as much with the heart as the head, was a primary reason Couch chose Kentucky.

Dave Baker recounts the final days leading up to Couch's decision:

Couch and I developed a relationship, and in some cases we talked several times a week. Not once, though, did the subject of whether or not he should come to Kentucky ever come up. I always just had a feeling that when it came right down to it, that's what would happen.

The last time I saw Tim before his decision was the Monday before Christmas week. Leslie County was having its football banquet and the folks in Hyden asked me to emcee the event. The guest speaker was Heisman Trophy winner Paul Hornung. A good friend of Bill Curry's, Hornung all but came out and said that every one of Tim's dreams could come true by staying home and playing for the Cats.

Afterward, we went over to the Couch house. It seemed to be filled with more people than the cafeteria held for the banquet. It was there that I told Tim and his dad that once they had made their minds up, whatever the decision, to let me know and I'd be happy to set up any sort of news conference or announcement. The only advice I gave was that, with the Kentucky-Louisville basketball game being played the next Saturday in Lexington, and *if* a young man was ready to make an announcement of such significance, he could count on every writer, reporter and camera in the state to already be there.

In Lexington, it began to appear more and more that Couch coming to Kentucky was a foregone conclusion. In Knoxville, however, the mood was likewise upbeat, especially for David Cutcliffe.

"Well, I'll tell you," Cutcliffe says. "I thought I *did* have him. Days before the Saturday morning announcement, I thought it was done—and for some good reasons. Things changed quickly at the end there, but I think *he* probably thought he was going to Tennessee for awhile. I had good reasons to believe that. But things changed."

Ultimately, they changed while Tim Couch sat in the pickup truck, motor running so he could stay warm, father inside and awake so he could learn the decision. Elbert Couch never came out and told his son what to do, but it was obvious where his heart resided.

"I guess it's every parent's dream in this state to have a son play for the University of Kentucky—but I didn't push him to go anywhere," Elbert says. "I kinda stayed in the background. But I did do some things that helped. I told him that if he got down there he'd be taken care of in the future. I mean, people in Lexington love football. And after it's over with, after you get your degree or whatever, if you want to stay in Kentucky ... where do you want to live when your football career is over? And Tim wants to live here in Kentucky."

Elbert Couch wanted his son to make the decision on his own. At the same time he wanted to have a back-up plan in place. Elbert had no doubt that his son could achieve his goals, but what if there was an injury? Who would make sure that Tim was taken care of? The answer, in Elbert's mind, was easy: the people of his home state.

And that's what it came down to in the middle of that cold December night.

"I was sitting here at about 3 o'clock in the morning worrying my butt off. Couldn't go to sleep," Elbert says. "So Tim goes out to the garage, out there with his truck runnin'."

Finally, Tim came back into the house.

He was wearing a UK cap and a UK shirt that he hadn't worn out to the garage.

"Tim, does this mean you've seen something?" Elbert asked.

Tim Couch grinned. "Yeah, dad," he said. "Go ahead and make the phone call. I'm going to Kentucky."

A hotline should be so busy. Elbert called Bill Curry, waking him. Then he called some friends. "Lynn and Bear and those guys," Elbert says. "I told them I'd pick them up at 7 in the morning. We all met down at the restaurant, had some coffee and headed to Lexington for the press conference."

Dave Baker had held a room at the Radisson Hotel just in case, but had heard nothing Friday night and resigned himself to the notion that nothing would happen that Saturday. He was waiting to go to Rupp Arena for the Kentucky-Louisvillle game when his pager began to vibrate. After calling the Couches and getting the word, he raced to

WKYT-TV and broke into regular programming with the news that Couch would announce at a noon news conference that he was coming to Kentucky. By the time he got to the hotel, virtually every TV station in Lexington and Louisville was already there. All of them broadcast Couch's announcement on live TV.

Word had spread like wildfire. Thousands of fans who were on their way downtown for the basketball game suddenly jammed their way into the press conference site, where a partition had been removed to transform two ballrooms into a large hall. What had started as a clever way to get extensive media attention had exploded into a frenzy of celebration.

"It was the most exciting thing that's ever happened to us—besides our two boys being born," Elbert says. "It was just an amazing feat. Everybody was just standing there. I'll never forget Joanne Oliver. She was from Louisville and she said, 'Tim, you sure look good in blue,' because he had on that blue cap and blue shirt. I just didn't know it was going to be that big of a deal."

It was big enough to take the UK-Louisville basketball game off the top of the front of the page of the sports section the next day. What in the name of bluegrass was happening? Football fever in the midst of one of Kentucky's most intense hoops rivalries? As Couch left the press conference and walked across the raised pedway in downtown Lexington, moving into the lobby of the Hyatt Regency and then into Rupp Arena itself, his progression carried the ambiance of a heavyweight champion walking to the ring. A sea of people parted as he walked by. They yelled and whooped. They took snapshots. They asked for autographs.

Most of all, they cheered with an undercurrent of hope that this announcement would herald a new era in Kentucky football.

Down in Knoxville, a much different story was playing out.

"I talked to his grandmother Saturday morning," David Cutcliffe says. "She's the one who informed me of the decision. I'd visited with Tim a few days earlier, and I was really taken by surprise.

"To be honest with you, it depressed me so much that it probably ended up being the best Christmas my family had—because to get out of that depression, I went out and spent more money than I should have. I just had to go Christmas shopping. My wife said, 'Good gosh! What have you done?'" I said, 'Well, I just had to do *something*.' I mean, I truly was down. I cared a lot about the youngster and his family. That happens in recruiting. It was right before Christmas and I didn't want to be Ebeneezer Scrooge, so I went and spent more money than I had at the time, to just get me in the Christmas spirit."

Meanwhile, Kentucky fans were celebrating a Couch under their tree. The Deuce, however, was to soon discover that a firm decision doesn't insure a trip down the smoothest road.

4

The Year of Living Aimlessly

When Tim Couch arrived on the University of Kentucky campus in 1996, Bill Curry was struck by the intense aura of anticipation surrounding his new player. What he sensed was an electricity that arced well beyond hope and straight to hosannas.

"I'm not exaggerating when I say that Tim Couch was somewhere above and beyond Daniel Boone and Abraham Lincoln in the mind of Kentuckians," Curry says. "I'm not kidding. I'm not using that as metaphor. That's a fact."

It is *not* a fact that Curry cast himself in the role of John Wilkes Booth—although a growing legion of Kentucky fans seemed to suspect as much as a season awash in controversy took its curious course. When it finally came to a merciful end, Bill Curry was no longer Kentucky's coach and Tim Couch was nearly no longer a Kentucky player.

What in the name of smash mouth football happened?

The answer, in part, lies in the question itself. Instead of an emphasis on finesse and airy-fairy airways, football to Curry is fundamentally a game of guts, grunts and ground attack. He was not a caricature in that regard—the man is too well read and too well rounded to suffer much from myopia in any aspect of life—but his basic, no-frills approach to football surely played a part in the events of '96.

Still, it's not an easy mystery to unravel. Curry, as we will later see, explains at length much of his thinking. UK athletics director C.M. Newton, his boss and friend, will say that he agrees with Curry's rationale given the conditions he faced. The Couch family won't, of course, and that's understandable as well.

The key plot points to the mystery are well known: Curry, putting his faith in associate head coach and offensive coordinator Elliot Uzelac, stuck with an option offense more suited to the talents of Billy Jack Haskins—an inspirational junior quarterback who made up with grit what he might have lacked in sheer talent.

Saying he wanted to protect Couch from having too much thrown at him too soon, Curry used him sparingly as UK lost six of its first seven games—and then failed to use him at all in three consecutive wins after Newton announced in October that Curry would be fired at season's end. Couch surfaced again, but only briefly, in the season finale, a 56-10 loss at Tennessee. Forced to run the option when he did get in and rarely throwing except in obvious passing situations, Couch spent the year being roughed up and ridiculed by opposing defenses.

Ask former Florida defensive back Lawrence Wright, now with the Cincinnati Bengals, what memories he has of

Couch that freshman season, and Wright laughs. "I don't have *any*. He didn't exist then," Wright says. "All I know is, our defensive line kept slamming him."

Couch produced season stats that fairly limped: 32 of 84 passes (38 percent) for 276 yards and one touchdown, with a long pass of 27 yards. In his junior year, Couch would pass for 300 or more yards in every game. As a freshman, he didn't reach 300 for the entire season.

More than Lincoln or Boone, Couch began the season as a living, breathing version of Luke Skywalker in the minds of Kentucky fans—a flight-ready hotshot come to rescue Planet Big Blue from the black hole of football mediocrity. You don't search long to find Darth Vader in this scenario. It was Uzelac—his decisions a dark mask of inscrutability that first had fans mystified, then peeved, then irate. Mostly, they were just mystified.

"That was Bill's phrase all the time, too, wasn't it," Elbert Couch says, and he can chuckle in retrospect. "Well, I stayed mystified the whole year."

"I just told him to hang in there," Janice Couch says. "It was awfully tough on him, because he hadn't been through that kind of thing before."

"I can't explain it," Greg Couch says. "I don't know what they were thinking, but it wasn't the right thing."

"I don't have any regrets about the decisions we made," Bill Curry says. "And I don't have any resentment toward people who were critical. That just goes with the territory. You make the decision based on all the information you have at the moment, you go out and play, and you do the best you can."

On the eve of the '96 campaign, an allure of mystery hovered over two-a-days. Curry had changed his policy and called for a media blackout of all practices. What was going on with all that secrecy? "I remember wondering if he wasn't revamping the offense completely and ready to start Couch in the first game," says Billy Reed, a columnist with the *Lexington Herald-Leader* and writer for *Sports Illustrated*.

Never happened.

In the season opener against arch-rival Louisville, Haskins started and Kentucky jumped to a 7-0 lead after a 62-yard punt return by Kio Sanford set up a 6-yard touchdown run by Ray McLaurin. U of L, however, scored 17 unanswered points in the second quarter. When the deficit grew to 24-7 in the third quarter, Curry called on Couch.

The kid began to move the team—and, late in the period, he looped a 20-yard pass to Isaac Curtis, Jr., who caught it on the run in the end zone as the ball carried perfectly over the outstretched hands of a U of L defender. When the ball was in flight, a Louisville assistant in the press box coaches booth could be heard screaming, "No, no, no!" When it was caught, the distraught coach threw something in disgust that shattered the booth's glass window.

His angst—and the sound of disintegrating glass—was lost in the roar of the crowd. They'd come to see Tim Couch, and he'd delivered. It was the first touchdown pass of his career. Who could have guessed it would be his last of the season?

Couch's throw drew Kentucky within 24-14, but Louisville—which wound up with two touchdowns scored directly by its defense and 10 more points after two blocked punts—scored 14 more points in the final quarter to win, 38-14.

Couch's debut seemed to herald the likelihood of more playing time—if not a starting role. He'd injected the only life in Kentucky's offense after its early score, and though his stats—8 of 20 passing for 101 yards—were hardly earth shattering, they showed promise. Couch had also displayed that trademark poise in the pocket. Nobody could doubt his ability to throw the ball, at any distance or speed. He had the touch. He also had the crowd. There was a palpable air of excitement each time he came into a game as the buzz in Commonwealth Stadium exploded into thunder with each completion. Often, even a miss would be accompanied by an audible "ooh!"—the pass admired for the sheer audacity of its trajectory and thrust.

There wasn't a doubt among them that the kid had the right stuff.

Not that it much mattered. Things got real bad, real quick. In UK's second game at Cincinnati, a team they'd beaten 33-14 the previous year, the Wildcats fell behind 14-0 in the first quarter and trailed 21-3 at the half. Held to just 173 yards in total offense, UK lost 24-3. When Couch entered the game in the second quarter, he mostly ran the option. He would attempt only four passes, completing none.

"We beat him up pretty good," says Artrell Hawkins, who was in the UC secondary that day. "He got sacked a bunch. I remember seeing him take his helmet off late in the game, not too happy. It wasn't really significant to me at the time, but obviously the option offense isn't him. At the time, though, I figured he just wasn't as good as people were saying he was."

Hawkins, like Wright a Cincinnati Bengals player now, said this the day after watching Couch's impressive NFL debut in the exhibition game on ABC's "Monday Night Football."

"And when I saw him, that's the one thought I had," Hawkins says, "that this was the same freshman quarterback at Kentucky that I thought wasn't a player three years earlier."

So soured were Tim Couch's parents by what was happening on the field that day in Cincinnati that they left the game at halftime and drove 110 miles to Richmond to watch their other son, Greg, play for Eastern Kentucky.

While the loss to Cincinnati soured Kentucky fans on the season, it conversely raised their level of expectation that Curry would scrap the option and let the kid fling it. UK was 0-2 and its offense was anemic. What was left to lose?

"CUT THE DEUCE LOOSE!" shouted the words on a large white sheet placed strategically in Commonwealth Stadium for the next game, against Indiana—but again Haskins started and again the offense stayed mostly to the ground. In a game most notable for its contribution to somnambulism, Kentucky was the first to awaken, winning 3-0 on a field goal with 14 seconds to play. Couch completed only two of eight passes for 19 yards, but he was behind the game-winning drive, executing a pitch to wideout Quentin McCord on a reverse that went 31 yards to set up the field goal.

And then, in the fourth game of the season, Tim Couch got the first start of his career.

Problem was, he had to do it against top-ranked Florida—in Gainesville, and in the notorious "Swamp," where Florida loses once every millennium. It was about the worst possible place for a football debutante to spread his wings—particularly when those wings were already severely clipped by the option offense.

Dave Baker, on hand to do color for the UK radio network and also report for his television station, remembers how he got the news:

When Kentucky plays in Gainesville, they usually stay about 45 minutes away from all the pre-game drunkenness and noise, opting for a motel in the quiet horse country of Ocala. The game was being televised by CBS, which meant a late (3:45 p.m.) kickoff time. As I normally do in situations like that, I went for a jog of three miles. As I returned to the hotel, who do I run into but Elliot Uzelac, soaking with sweat after his own run.

"Well, your man's going to get the ball today," Uzelac said, meaning Couch would start. "He's looked good, and you've got to get him in there sometime."

"Elliott," I said, "I'm no football coach, but why would you do it here on the road in front of the best defense in the country and the loudest fans in the country?"

"Hey," Uzelac said, "in this situation, there'll actually be less pressure on him than if he was starting at home."

I was dumbfounded. Were they just setting him up to stop the ground swell of Couch support, or had these guys really misread the situation even worse than I thought they had?

I wondered, too, about the widespread scuttlebutt—though each coach has denied it publicly—that Curry and

Florida coach Steve Spurrier aren't exactly on each other's Christmas card list. The story goes that when Curry became head coach at Georgia Tech, there was an offensive hotshot—none other than Spurrier—from the previous regime who hoped to remain on Curry's new staff. According to a lot of insiders familiar with the situation, Spurrier has never let it go. As if he didn't have enough motivation going, now Spurrier could focus on throwing everything he could at Curry's prize freshman quarterback to get in yet another "statement."

If true, the statement was made in capital letters. There were 85,422 boisterous fans that day, itching to see the kid be thrown to the Gators. They got what they sought.

Florida would go on to win the national championship that season, and they looked every bit the part in tearing into Kentucky. Still saddled with the option and facing a Florida defense that swarmed and out-quicked Kentucky's line, Couch was pummeled. He was also intercepted on his first series. He finished six of 18 for 13 yards. Trailing 41-0 by halftime, UK lost 65-0.

By now, Tim Couch was having serious reservations about his choice of schools—and pondering a new one.

"He wouldn't have done it in the middle of a season," Elbert Couch says, "on account of his teammates. But he was already talking to me about transferring."

Back in Lexington, fans and media were having serious reservations about Curry's approach. Critical columns and articles began to appear more frequently. Former Heisman Trophy winner and Notre Dame/Green Bay Packers standout Paul Hornung—a native Louisvillian who followed Kentucky and was a friend of Curry's—began to publicly question Curry's strategy. Like most people, he was aghast. What in the world was going on?

The next week, the questions only grew larger and louder.

Rather than let Couch get more playing time and regain some lost confidence, Curry didn't play him at all at Alabama. Kentucky fought valiantly and was tied 7-7 after two quarters, but was buried under a 28-point Bama explosion in the third period and fell, 35-7.

Curry said Couch didn't play because he had tendinitis in his throwing arm. But on the sidelines, Couch spent the entire game throwing a football with other players. Nobody saw him favoring the arm or showing any sign of physical pain. He must have tossed it a hundred times. TV cameras would focus on him occasionally, the announcers speculating that maybe he was getting ready to come in.

Instead, the odd little drama on the sidelines began to suggest another purpose. With each throw, Couch seemed to be acting out one of those videos of captured American pilots, the one where the pilot is trotted out on camera by the enemy and tries to blink his eyes in morse code to get out the real story of his situation.

Couch said little after the game, only confirming in a voice just this side of monotone that he'd felt fine and had been ready to play. His face masked any concern. But when the video cam lights were turned off and the notepads were put away, Rena Vicini—UK's assistant athletic director for media relations—saw something else. "It was like he was white as sheet and totally without emotion," she says. "It was like he was dead."

Dave Baker recalls:

I went up to him for a TV interview and said, "What's the deal with the elbow?" Couch said, "Oh, it's fine. I had one day this week when it was kind of sore, but as of now it's doing great."

"So you felt you were ready to play today, no problem?" I asked.

"Oh yeah, definitely," Couch said. "I felt like I would be ready, but it was Coach's decision and he made a good decision. Billy Jack came in and played well. If anything would have happened, I would have been ready."

That was on camera. Typical Tim. Downplaying it all. But at the end of the tunnel outside the locker room, away from other reporters and cameras, I spoke with him alone, trying to get to the bottom of the mystery. Had something gone on in practice that week? Was there some incident? Had he seen it coming? When Tim Couch answered, I was not prepared for the side of himself that he showed. No more quiet confidence, no more unruffled persona.

"I don't know what's going on," he confided. He shook his head in disbelief. His eyes began to mist up. "They just came to me at breakfast and said they were going with Billy Jack."

It was the only time I had ever seen him that way. He seemed puzzled, with no way to turn. He seemed lost.

So was Kentucky's season. The Wildcats were 1-4. In Commonwealth Stadium, the "CUT THE DEUCE LOOSE" sign still conveyed its forlorn message. Only now, there was a growing realization that The Deuce might cut himself loose—from UK football forever. The crowd had grown surly by now. Boos rained down on the coaching staff with increasing frequency. In the next game, a home contest against South Carolina, Couch did get more playing time. He came off the bench to hit 11 of 23 passes for 102 yards, but Kentucky blew a 14-3 halftime lead and fell 25-14. Next, at LSU, Couch started but Haskins again played the bulk of the game, hitting 13 of 17 passes for 172 yards. Couch attempted four passes, completing two. UK lost, 41-14.

The Wildcats were 1-6. They had lost 10 of their last 12 games over a two-season stretch. A couple of days later, C.M. Newton announced that Bill Curry would not return as Kentucky's coach in 1997.

"I never second guessed Bill Curry's coaching," Newton says. "To me, Bill is an outstanding, knowledgeable football coach. He's demonstrated that over and over. The concern I had was that we had made a commitment in recruiting Tim that we were going to change some things offensively to accommodate him, and that was a concern—because in his freshman year, that change never really occurred. And I can understand that, because Bill put us in the mode that he thought would give us the best chance to win that year. But as far as making the coaching change because of Tim Couch, that was never the case. It was more because we'd just reached a point where we weren't progressing."

Nevertheless, it's also true that it came at a time when Couch was highly likely to leave Kentucky—perhaps even willing to sit out two years to play at Tennessee—had Curry stayed.

"He was going to handle it differently than I did at Eastern," Greg Couch says. "He was going to transfer. Had Curry stayed, he would be gone, I'm pretty sure."

The warning signs had been everywhere. At one point, Kentucky basketball coach Rick Pitino called in Couch to give him a pep talk and try to help him deal with the situation, adjust to campus life and stay committed to Kentucky.

At some point after Curry was fired, Newton sat down with both Tim and Elbert Couch.

"The only thing I'm going to ask," Newton told them, "is not to do anything or even think about anything until we name a new coach. Give us a chance to get this coach in place, and it's going to be someone that I think you're going to want to play for, and the rest of these guys are going to want as well."

The Couches assured Newton that they'd wait and see.

As the rest of Curry's lame duck season played out, a strange thing happened. Geeked on emotion for their fallen coach, who would lead them the rest of the way despite the announcement, the Wildcats won their next three games—over Georgia (24-17), Mississippi State (24-21) and Vanderbilt (25-0). In a move that appeared all too telling to Kentucky fans who wondered if the kid wasn't being intentionally shunned, Couch didn't take a single snap in those three victories. Not until the season-ending 56-10 loss to Tennessee did he surface again. He threw seven passes. He completed three. For 21 yards.

In his first season, Couch played in seven games and started in two—both times on the road. Through it all, he never lost his temper publicly, never took advantage of the many opportunities he had to vent his frustrations and criticisms. It was not only Tim's nature not to do so, it was also smart.

"Yes," says Greg Couch, "because a lot of those players still believed in Uzelac's system, and in Billy Jack and the offensive scheme. I think he did the right thing."

"You don't really talk," Elbert Couch says. "You do by doing. My superintendent always told me, 'Make sure that your brain is engaged before kicking your mouth into gear,' and that was probably the best advice I ever got."

Advice that Tim Couch heeded as well. He would do by doing. He just had no idea that it would take a season of controversy, a coach's firing and a second decision to stay at Kentucky to give him the chance.

Why did Bill Curry play his cards the way he did?

First, it is important to remember Curry's background and mindset. An undersized lineman who nevertheless rose to become a starting center for the Green Bay Packers during some of their finest years, Curry had accomplished much through determination, guile and guts. To him, "smash mouth" was no idle phrase. It implied a belief that games were to be won through pride, hard work and passionate commitment to the basics of blocking, tackling and running. You beat the other guy by out-doing him in the basics. It was old school, and it had served him well.

However, two truths come to mind: Never get into a ground war in Southeast Asia, and never get into a game of "smash mouth" in the Southeastern Conference unless your smashers are bigger and better than the opponents'—lest ye become the smashee. Given Kentucky's obvious disadvantage in terms of overall talent, size and depth, smash mouth alone was a flawed strategy.

The result was that, in seven seasons, Curry compiled a meager 26-52 record and had only two winning seasons—6-5 in 1989 and 6-5 in 1993, although a heartbreaking, last-seconds 14-13 loss to Clemson in the Peach Bowl leveled that team's record to 6-6. The next season, 1994, UK would sink to 1-10. In 1995 the Wildcats finished 4-7. Ironically, however, the 1995 season that immediately preceded Couch's arrival served to keep alive the smash mouth creed.

That same year, Uzelac installed a one-back offense predicated on the running game. The result was that tailback Moe Williams rushed for a school-record 1,600 yards and then left early for the NFL. Moreover, five of the seven losses came by 10 points or less—an encouraging sign. Meanwhile, Haskins had taken over at quarterback for the last nine games, four of them wins. He passed for 1,176 yards and set a school record by completing 60.4 percent of his passes.

More than that, however, was the heart he displayed. Despite playing with a separated left shoulder over the last three games, Haskins soldiered on, and against Tennessee he nearly engineered an upset. His 47-yard touchdown run over, through and around a host of Vol defenders was so remarkable that it was nominated for an ESPY award as the year's greatest play in college football. The run came in the fourth quarter to give Kentucky a 31-27 lead. His shoulder hit during the run, Haskins had to come out of the game shortly afterward because the pain was so great that he couldn't lift his arm to pass. Tennessee came back to escape with a 34-31 victory.

It was not easy, then, for Curry to forsake the offense he preferred, let alone relegate Haskins to a background role. Why not build on the promise the offense had shown, not to mention the hard-nosed leadership of Haskins, and let Couch develop gradually without exposing him to too much too soon? If that underestimated the uncommon maturity of Tim Couch, it at least seemed a sound approach on paper. Still, sooner or later you'd have to commit to an offense more suited to the kid's remarkable throwing abilities. In Couch's freshman season, Curry apparently believed he could retain the option and still make room for the passing game.

A quote in the 1996 UK media guide is revealing. "We've just scratched the surface with what we can do in this offense," Curry said. "We can throw the ball more while keeping the same emphasis on a physical brand of running the football." Such was the background as Couch entered the scene. And such was the quandary Curry faced.

"Quandary is a good word," Curry says. "And then you add the fact that there was so much expectation regarding Tim with all that was thrust on his shoulders. So how do I keep from just burying him, and how do I do justice to this offensive line that's going to be good, but ... I mean, it was obvious that we were going to be pretty good at some point during that year, but it was also obvious that we weren't going to be good in the beginning. So how do you mingle all that? Well, we worked at it and we did the best we could."

In an ideal world, would Curry have redshirted Couch?

"I think in an ideal world Bill Curry is redshirted as a freshman, as are most other guys who have a little talent and a lot of work to do," Curry answers. "But I don't think Tim Couch could have sat out a year. He was just too good. The tough thing always with a player like that—especially if you have a Billy Jack Haskins, who's a proven quantity and the team captain and a leader and you have a very young, very poor offensive unit in the beginning of the year, where you know the quarterback's going to take a beating—what do you do with a 17-, 18-year-old who's *got to play*? I mean, you try to find a way to play him, and that's exactly what we did.

"The other thing you have to consider is the whole football team—all these other freshmen and all these other players who are also critically important. So, how do you intermingle all of that? It's a very complex matrix."

It was a complexity that Hal Mumme would eliminate within days of being named coach in December of 1996. After looking at films, Mumme said Couch would be his starting quarterback come spring practice of 1997. Haskins transferred to Delaware. Which begs the question: Had Curry not been fired, would Billy Jack Haskins still have been No. 1 entering the spring?

"I saw it developing as a competitive situation, which is what I promised both of them," Curry says. "I mean, you've got to be careful what you promise people, because folks expect you to keep your word. So I promised Billy Jack when all that recruiting of Tim started, 'I'm not going to give your job away before the guy even gets on campus.' And I promised Tim, 'You'll have a chance to take the job from Billy Jack or whoever else has it, and it will be a fair competition.'

"Now, when you start into fair competition, the players almost always do not regard the competition as fair—except for the one who gets the job. He thinks it's fair. Nobody else thinks it's fair, but that's a fact of life.

"I don't know whether Tim thought the competition was fair or not, but I thought it was. I tried to get him in there when I thought he had a chance to succeed and help us win, and I tried to play Billy Jack when I thought he had a chance to help us win and succeed.

"And, adding in all the other factors that were the (team) rules … and I don't talk about who followed rules and who didn't publicly, but that included class attendance and tutoring attendance. I tried to be even-handed with all the freshmen, knowing all the time that we had a folk hero on our team—and heaven knows Tim earned it. I mean, what he did in high school was unprecedented. So I mean, he deserved to be as admired as he was, but I'm not sure any youngster deserves to have that much pressure on him.

"So I tried to take as much pressure off him as I could, but at the same time give him a chance to succeed. It was a challenging situation for everybody."

It's no secret, of course, that Couch's favorite classroom was the football field. Not that he didn't enjoy some of his courses. He particularly liked the semester spent working with disadvantaged Lexington youths as part of his major in social work. Nevertheless, many of his classes held little allure. "Like algebra," he told Terry Frei of *The Sporting News*. "When are you going to walk into a bank and have somebody ask you, 'What is the value of x?' "

Curry understood the single-mindedness that Couch had for football. But, being one who demanded strict adherence to his rules regarding class work, he found himself confronting that single-mindedness. Curry understands how intense focus has served Tim Couch well, but his approach to players, and freshmen in particular, was to demand more of them off the field.

"It (single-mindedness) can be a curse when you're a freshman in college," Curry says. "When you're in the NFL, it's most assuredly a blessing. I've never known a great NFL player who wasn't obsessed. I've known some decent ones who hung on, who weren't obsessed, who had to go out and get drunk and do the foolishness. But I've never known a truly great one, a Starr or a Unitas or a Mike Curtis or a John Mackey or Willie Davis who wasn't obsessed with his craft.

"That kind of focus is an advantage for a pro, but when you're a freshman in college and you're expected to go to tutoring, you're expected to go to class, and you're expected to show up at the training room at a certain time, and you're expected to show up at the press conference and answer the tough questions about why did the coach play you and why didn't he play you... that's hard when you're 17 or 18 years old.

"So, it can be a mixed blessing at that time in your life. And that's when Tim and I and all the other freshmen who ever played for me had to sit down and talk about it. 'OK now, I promised your mom...' because she didn't ask me but one question, and it was, 'Are you going to see that he gets his education and goes to class?' And I said yes. So I'm going to do that, and 'Tim, you have to go to all these things.'

"Now, I didn't want to hear it when I was a freshman in college, and Tim wasn't real excited about it, either. But he wasn't the first guy who couldn't get excited about all that other stuff."

As C.M. Newton notes: "Tim got a little bit of a bad rap in some things—academically and that type thing. But Tim did what he needed to do academically. Will he ever graduate? Probably not. I don't know if I had 47 or 48 million dollars if I'd come back and finish school, either. Now he may. I hope he does. But that becomes a moot point at this point in time."

Newton likewise understands the position Curry faced with his loyalty to Haskins and the promises he made to both Haskins and Couch.

"I think Bill was exactly right," he says. "Bill had recruited both those gentlemen, and I think the way he played that out was exactly the way he should have—to be truthful and loyal to the entire team. And that was part of the dilemma, because what you had was a veteran quarterback who everybody had to love.

"Billy Jack Haskins ... what he did here was tremendous. He gave himself totally to the type offense they ran. He played hurt. He was a great leader. He had the total support of the veteran players. And then you have a young talent who's kind of a gun, who has the total support of the younger players. The split in a team that that can create ... Bill Curry could not have afforded that. He would have had to let the competition between the two take place on the field."

It was the reason, Newton says, why a Hal Mumme could make the hard choice without letting it play out on the field, while Curry couldn't.

"A new coach coming in isn't bound to that promise," he says. "A new coach can say, 'Hey, I'm going to handle this a certain way.' And of the people I talked to for the coaching position, Hal was the only one who indicated that he'd make the decision himself. I brought that question up with every one I interviewed: 'How do you handle this situation?' And I gave them an accurate description of Billy Jack: a talented youngster, a gutsy, great competitor, great leader. And here you've also got a young guy who's got unusual ability. So I'd ask them, 'How will you address that?' Every one of them gave the same answer that Bill did: 'We'll take them out there, we'll start them out even, we'll let them emerge.'

"Hal, on the other hand, said, 'There *won't* be any quarterback controversy. I've never had one and I won't have one. I'll make the decision. And I'll make that on the basis of studying the tapes and studying the film, and when I get there, I'm going to name the quarterback.' "

Given that Curry could not make a decision in the same fashion, the obvious question looms: With the benefit of hindsight, does he think Couch would have won the job from Haskins in the spring of 1997? Curry pauses for several seconds before answering.

"Well, that's a very loaded question," he says. "I mean, I don't know. I think because Billy Jack is so competitive ... Billy Jack's competitive juices and his ability to rise to the occasion—I mean, that run against Tennessee was very symbolic; that's a good metaphor for the man. Billy Jack just did things you didn't think he could do. He seemed to pull things out of his hat at the darndest times, and he did it all the way to the end.

"So I don't know what he might have done, but I think it would have been extremely difficult for anybody in America to hold off Tim for a second year. We would have gone into spring practice with a full package that suited

Tim's talents, and a package that suited Billy Jack's—and we would have seen what was best for the team."

If Couch had emerged, would the offensive scheme have changed dramatically?

"Yes. Sure," Curry says. "We already had the shotgun in, which we had not emphasized with Billy Jack for obvious reasons, and we would have evolved toward a Tim Couch offense as three things happened—number one, as the team developed so we had the protection, so that somebody could pass protect one on one.

"The second thing that needed to happen was that the young quarterback had to grow into this speed of football, which Tim was doing.

"And the third thing was that some receivers had to emerge who could go get the ball. We had a very young, very raw Craig Yeast, who would come and tug at my shirt and say, 'Coach, I'm very uptight today.' And I'd say, 'OK, Craig, you're going to be a great player. Go out and relax and catch the ball.' I mean, we were really dealing with that kind of thing, which is what you have to do while young people grow up.

"So we were trying to make all that happen simultaneously with our first responsibility, which was to try to win the game. When you go into a game and you've got two weapons—one of them is an option offense and one of them is a drop back pass offense—you can't run everything in every game. So you pick the things that give you the best chance to win that week. And then you polish them, you get in the game and you run 'em."

As the frustration of the 1996 season mounted, a number of people began to wonder if Tim Couch had become a pawn in a game of mounting criticism by fans and media and stubbornness on the part of the coaches—in particular, Uzelac—to do things their way. Some wondered if decisions might have been made merely out of the coaches deciding to show who was in charge. In his darker moments, Greg Couch, for one, thinks it might have been the case.

"They took a lot of that out on Tim, even though he had nothing to do with it," he says. "I mean, a lot of people wanted to see him play. They'd read so much about him in high school. They put a lot of pressure on the coaches to put him in. So they put him in his first game (as a starter) against Florida, the number one team in the country, for no other reason than to make him look bad. I mean, had they thrown the ball a little bit and done some other things it may have been a little different, but they put him in a situation where he couldn't be successful. I lost a lot of respect for them at that time—to see the way they treated him after that, even though he had nothing to do with it."

Curry, however, says such was never the case. And there's nothing in the man's character to suggest that his decisions were based in part on spite.

"If you get into that as a coach, you're allowing the thoughts of people who don't do this for a living to control what you do," he says. "You can't let yourself respond to that either way—in other words, 'I'm going to stick with my system' or 'I'm going to change my system' just as a reactionary thing to what somebody else thinks. That is clearly the most stupid and the most dishonest policy a coaching staff could possibly take.

"So let me give you an answer: No, that's not what we did.

"What Elliot was trying to do was what he always tries to do, which is to win the game. And he would have done that with any weapon at his disposal. Elliot's always had, shall we say, a perception problem. Wherever he's been, people haven't always understood, but his heart was in the right place—if what you really wanted to do was win the game for Kentucky. If what you really wanted was to get a certain player in the game, then you might never like Elliot Uzelac, because what he was going to do is sit down, spend 90 hours a week and figure out the best possible way to win this game on offense. And that's why he's had so much success on offense wherever he's been. But he's also had people angry at him wherever he's been. It's kind of Elliot's nature."

The irony to the situation, of course, is that, had Curry elected to play Couch exclusively and tailor the offense to him, he might have saved his job even with a similar record. Has Curry considered that?

"I think when you coach football, very early in your career as a head coach you've got to decide, am I going to be honest and try to do what's best for this program and these student athletes, or am I going to try to save my job when that seems like the thing to do?" Curry says. "Once you make that decision, you don't have to face that monster any more.

"I would love to have saved my job. We're all selfish. I would love to have kept that staff intact. But the job description doesn't include that. The job description says, follow all NCAA rules, graduate every player and win—and win all the games if you're in the SEC, Okay? [He chuckles.] So that's what we tried to do. And I'll let that stand as my answer.

"Whether it was Tim or any other individual, if you get caught up in what is going to accrue to the benefit of one individual or to the head coach at the expense of the program, or possibly at the expense or at the integrity of the program, I don't know how you sleep at night. I really, really don't."

Since that fateful season, Curry has not spoken with Couch.

"I would love to see him and would love to talk with him, but I really don't feel like it's been appropriate," he says. "It wouldn't have been appropriate for me to sort of horn in on his success. I've intentionally not done that, but I've been happy for him, and I'm really proud of him."

Elbert Couch reflects on The Year of Living Aimlessly and now sees the good that resulted.

"It wasn't the best thing at the time," he says, "but you look back and realize that Tim hadn't faced a lot of adversity before, and that year put him through some. He went down there expecting Coach Curry to change the offense from the running type game. Tim was kind of disappointed. So were a lot of us, I guess. You know, I was mad for awhile. But I got over it. Everything's worked out perfectly for Tim. Hal Mumme came in and just threw the heck out of the ball. Tim loved it."

For Hal Mumme, the feeling was mutual. No better pairing could have emerged than this, the Young Gun and the Young Coach, Skywalker and Solo, each itching for an Air Raid.

In retrospect, maybe their convergence *was* in the stars.

5

Enter the Parrothead

It was a cool, clear October night—the eve of Kentucky's 1997 game with Alabama. Hal Mumme, the new coach, stood beside Tim Couch, the born again quarterback, in the parking lot of the hotel where the team stayed on nights before home games. As always, the players went outside in street clothes to run through some basic alignments and even jog through some plays. The starting quarterback never throws in this drill. He mostly stands beside the coach and they talk.

"Tim and I were standing there," Mumme says, "and we were looking at the stars up in the sky. It was just beautiful—a beautiful, clear fall night in Kentucky. We're standing there and I remembered this great quote from Shelby Foote's book on the Civil War. One of the chapters is about the stars and their courses. It talks about how Gettysburg was just fate. You know, how fate is going to control destiny and everything. And I told Tim about that.

"And then I said, 'You know, Tim, we're going to win this game tomorrow night. I can just feel it. I just think it's the stars and their courses.' And he was in total agreement. I mean, you could tell. You just had this sense about it, you know?"

A few days later, Mumme would choose—as he always does—a Jimmy Buffett song to play over top video highlights of the previous week's game on his television show. The night after the coach and quarterback had gawked at the universe above them and intuited victory, goalposts had fallen in Commonwealth Stadium. Kentucky had beaten Bama 40-34, its first win over the Crimson Tide in 75 years. Couch had thrown for 355 yards and four touchdowns—including the game-winner to Craig Yeast in overtime.

The coach, digging into his Buffett discography, found the music he wanted as a theme song to the highlights video.

He chose "Stars Fell on Alabama."

Hal Mumme did not arrive in Lexington with a white sport coat and a pink crustacean, but he might as well have. Suddenly, games in Commonwealth Stadium had Buffett music played through the PA during pre-game drills. Suddenly, there was a sense of fun, frolic and derring-do to go with the raised level of football performance. Suddenly, Kentucky had a coach who might as readily be spotted wearing a Panama hat as he would a blue cap. *"Lexington, Tranquility Base here. The Parrothead has landed."*

Had he ever. Emerging from the vapor of Division II football where anonymity was first team on the depth chart, Mumme brought his offensive genius, brought his intriguing mix of intellect and loosey-goosey wit, and brought his ability to build rapport, particularly with quarterbacks. It was exactly the kind of fresh blend of attitude—both fun-loving and fiery—that Kentucky's players in general, and Couch in particular, needed. Along with his ability to fashion audacity into offensive brilliance was his infectious persona. It helped lift the psychological burden of losing, of looking over the shoulder to see what awful thing was going to happen next—which had more or less become the trademark of UK football.

It was fitting—and maybe it *was* in the stars—that Hal Mumme and Tim Couch converge. They were two of a kind in many respects—particularly in attitude and approach to the game.

"They were like one person," says Rena Vicini, UK's assistant athletic director for media relations. "We went down to SEC Media Days in Birmingham (before Mumme's first season in 1997) and afterward we were flying back in a little private plane. I was sitting in the jump seat and feeling sleepy, but Hal and Tim kept talking about the offense—about x's and o's the entire time. I didn't sleep. I just listened to them. I didn't understand half of what they were saying, but they were finishing each other's sentences. And Tim was so excited. I mean, he doesn't act excited but you could just tell that he was totally sold and that they had the same brain. They clicked on every cylinder.

"What struck me was just how *relaxed* both were. I mean, you'd think that, new coach and a new quarterback, there would be a little 'mentor and student' kind of tension in that. But there was nothing."

"They got along great from day one," Greg Couch says. "They're both just kind of laid back people and they love what they do. Tim was excited. He knew he was going to be doing a lot of the things he'd done in high school and get the chance to be successful now."

C.M. Newton had likewise given Mumme a chance. He made his choice based on finding someone who could "press and shoot the threes and fast break on grass," as Newton—a former basketball player at Kentucky and a former coach at Alabama and Vanderbilt—put it. But he was equally swayed by Mumme's attitude regarding players.

"One of the questions I asked him was, 'What's your greatest strength as a football coach?'" Newton says. "And I asked each of the people I interviewed, all the way through: 'What's your major strength?' Each one of them in different ways would say organization, the scheme ... you know, the typical kind of coaching answers.

"I'll never forget Hal's answer. He looked right at me and he says, 'You know, I think the greatest strength I bring to the table is that I can remember what it's like to be 19 years of age.' Then he said, 'I've got a son, for example, that I would like to get up Saturday morning wanting to go out and mow the yard, do this, that and the other. He would much rather sit and watch 'Beavis and Butthead.' And then he said, 'The truth is, I'd rather watch 'Beavis and Butthead' with him than go out and do those things. I can remember what it's like. As a result, I think I have an ability to communicate with that age group, and really communicate with them where we understand each other.'

"I think that's one of his strengths. He does have that. He's firm. He's tough with discipline. But he understands that age group."

Dick Gabriel, sideline announcer for the UK radio network, discovered that firsthand in the 1997 game at Indiana, where Couch threw seven touchdowns in only three quarters as Kentucky romped, 49-7.

"There were three or four minutes to go," Gabriel says. "I turned around and Steve Moss goes, 'Hey, look at that!' I looked over, and there was Tim signing autographs. During the game. Signing autographs. After the game I was setting up the post-game show and talking to Hal—and mind you, I like Bill Curry, but I know Bill wouldn't have stood for that because he's just an old school kind of guy. Anyway, I said something to Hal about it. I said, 'Hey, I noticed some of your players signing autographs during the game.' He says, 'Yeah, who?' I said, 'Well, I don't want to say. I don't want to get anybody in trouble' And he says, 'I don't care. Tell me.' So I said, 'Well, Tim and Craig (Yeast).' And Hal says, 'Good! Let 'em have some fun!' "

Very little about Hal Mumme is conventional. It has served him well in developing his offense over the years, and in convincing Newton to make the gamble that a Division II coach could revive both Kentucky's program and Couch.

Mumme arrived in Lexington on December 2, 1996. One of his first acts was to announce that Couch was his starting quarterback.

There was a decent-sized ripple of protest from those in the Billy Jack Haskins camp, made all the more bitter by the fact that Haskins soon transferred. But it was nothing like what might have occurred had the Couch-Haskins question lingered through spring drills and simmered during the summer. The vast majority of Kentucky fans didn't want to see Couch submerged again. They wanted to see what he could do in a wide-open offense.

Nobody, of course, knew whether "Mummeball" would fly in the turbulent air of SEC football. Valdosta—where Mumme was 40-17-1 in five seasons at Valdosta State—isn't exactly Knoxville, in temperament or in the caliber of football played. If observers were shocked that Newton picked Mumme (and many of them openly voiced their doubts) rest assured that both Newton and Mumme recognized the brazenness of the act.

Newton has a favorite story regarding all that. It starts when he and assistant athletic director Larry Ivy visited the Mumme home late in the decision process.

"After we'd spent two or three hours together," Newton says, "and as Larry and I were leaving, Hal said, 'I just need to know. We're getting ready to go to the playoffs. Are you really serious about me? Can you really hire me at Kentucky?'

"I just told him, 'Hal, if you're the right guy, I've got balls enough to hire you. I'll assure you of that—*if* you're the right guy.' And he said, 'Well, that's all I need to know.'

"A few days later I called to offer him the job. June was there. He wasn't. So I told June. I'd gotten to know both of them because, to me, the wife is as important a part of this team as anybody. So I tried to talk to both of them together as much as possible. But I wanted to talk to Hal, and June said, 'Well, he's on his way home.' And I said, 'Well, I'm not going to hold you out any longer on this. I'm calling to offer him the job.' And she just said, 'That's wonderful.'

"About that same time, she said, 'He's coming in now. You tell him.' So he got on the phone and I said, 'Hal, I want you to be the coach at Kentucky and we'll get all the contract and stuff worked out.' We'd never talked contract. And I said, 'We'll get all that worked out, but I want you to be our coach.'

"There was a pause for a moment, and then Hal said, 'Boy, you really *do* have big balls!'

Newton breaks into laughter.

"And I said, 'Well, so do you. We're going to be in this together, honey, I'll tell ya.' "

Three years later, Newton still chortles over the exchange. Underneath the retelling of the punch line, though, a trace of nervous giddiness in his voice underscores the potentially bleak consequences each man had faced. Both Newton and Mumme would have been easy targets if the grand experiment failed.

There was also a personal crisis to face. Not long before Newton contacted him as a candidate for the Kentucky job, Hal learned that June had breast cancer. It was discovered during a routine checkup. She had the lump removed. When the tumor was diagnosed as malignant, she underwent a mastectomy. A few days later, Newton called to set up an interview. When Mumme hung up the phone, the first thing he did was ask his wife if he should tell Newton that he wasn't interested. Her health was more important to him. He would turn down the possibility of coaching at Kentucky if that's what she desired, but June Mumme wanted nothing of the sort. She told him to go for it.

She would undergo chemotherapy for the next several months, her hair falling out and pain a constant companion. In the early weeks after Mumme was hired, he would live out of a hotel in Lexington while June was still in Valdosta. In what should have been a period that was as heady as it was hectic, Mumme was on the phone to his wife three or four times a day, the weight of June's situation hanging heavily over both of them.

He was only able to visit her every three weeks or so. It was a difficult period—but they'd both made the choice. June Mumme writes eloquently of the close relationship she has with her husband in her book, *Play the Next Play*. Today, she is doing well. Doctors give her a 90 percent chance of survival.

When he was still just a candidate for the job, Mumme had borrowed film from Guy Morriss (then at Mississippi State; soon to become UK's offensive line coach) of Kentucky games "so I wouldn't be ignorant," Mumme says, "when I talked to C.M." He looked at film of games against Louisville, LSU and Florida. Even though Couch didn't play much, he stood out.

"I thought he was the best player they had," Mumme says. "There was one play that really impressed me. It was against LSU, a kind of bootleg they used to run in Curry's offense where Tim rolled to his right and got pressured by that big defensive lineman at LSU. Tim stiffarms the end. Then he's falling back on his back foot, but he kind of whips it sidearm about 20 yards downfield and hits the guy between the numbers. I think the receiver dropped it. But I just thought, 'This guy can move his feet.' And obviously he could throw the ball. There were several other plays where I thought, 'This guy can run our offense.'

"It was an easy decision. I was a little surprised at the debate it caused, although I understood it because of the geographical nature of the state. Obviously in Western Kentucky, Billy Jack would be the favorite and in Eastern

Kentucky, Tim would. It was convenient for me that Tim was so talented. Had they been real equal, it would probably have been a harder decision. It probably would have cost us a couple games because it would have taken longer for us to decide. But there wasn't any doubt in my mind as long as Tim was a good person. As soon as I got here, the first thing I did was start checking around on him a little bit."

Two or three days later, Mumme called in Couch.

"I sat him down and said, 'Do you want to be a starter in the SEC?' And he said yes. So I said, 'Well, this is a good place to be. You're going to be it. And the only way you can blow that is to not make your grades.' So he got after it in the classroom. The thought of him leaving never really came up. I'd heard about it from the media, but there was never any discussion about it between him and me."

Later, Mumme visited the Couch family in Hyden. It was Christmas Eve. Santa should be so skilled at appropriate gift-giving as Mumme was that night. He showed them Valdosta videos of his offense. Footballs danced in flight across the screen. He reassured them that Tim would have every opportunity to blossom. Then he got back in his car. And soon got lost in the mountains.

"We were re-recruiting the players, and after Tim we wanted to go see George Massey down in Lynch (about 30 miles from Hyden)," Mumme says. "Well, they gave us a shortcut to get back to I-75, and we got lost. (Assistant coach Mike) Fanoga was with me. Finally, at about one o'clock in the morning, we passed a sign that said WEL-COME TO VIRGINIA. I said, 'Mike, I think we're wrong.' So we took a right, the first place where you could take a right, and wound up on I-40 until we finally found I-75. I think we got back at six in the morning on Christmas Day."

Two years later, Hal Mumme would have a 12-11 record at Kentucky—modest by normal standards but highly significant against the backdrop of UK's past. His two-year record was the best start by a Kentucky coach in 43 years. His regular-season 7-4 record of 1998 was the best in 14 years—and it was a season in which UK scored more than 50 points in two consecutive games, the first time that had happened in 84 years. There was the win over Alabama in '97, the win at LSU in '98 (UK's first road win over a ranked team in 21 years) and a New Year's Day Bowl, Kentucky's first in 47 years. In 1997, UK was ranked sixth nationally in total offense, up from 109th the previous year.

There were Hal Mumme masks, Hal Mumme songs and—on the road running by the stadium—a street sign that said Hal Mumme Pass. "I didn't know if it was an honor or an order," he joked at the time. Mumme received contract extensions at the end of each season, and his overall salary jumped to third highest among SEC coaches at approximately $850,000 per year.

Couch, of course, was the key player behind the turnaround—along with Yeast, who became the leading pass receiver in SEC history. Some critics point out that Mumme only finished one game over .500 despite a quarterback just this side of Zeus, but what they neglect to note is that Mumme inherited a pool of defensive talent that was ankle deep, at best.

That first season, he had only two defensive ends who weighed more than 230 pounds. He shifted Dele Ali, a 213-pound senior, to the spot—Ali's third position change in as many years (he wound up starting). There were a dozen or so scholarship players on defense. A walk-on wound up starting. They were mostly small, relatively slow and clearly outnumbered.

In a telling example of just how drastic the situation was, Janet Graham of the *Kentucky Post* wrote that when defensive ends coach Tom Adams met with a group of potential candidates for the position that first year, he asked how many of them had not seen action at defensive end the previous season. "There were about 10 of them there," Adams told Graham, "and only two guys didn't raise their hands." It was a revolving door, manned by munchkins.

The result of this dearth of defensive help was that UK allowed almost 38 points per game in 1997 and finished last in nearly every SEC defensive statistical category. Kentucky's defense was improved in 1998, but the fact remains that, had Mumme had only reasonable defensive talent and depth when he first arrived, he'd likely have finished far better than 12-11. Defensive coordinator Mike Major points out that, on both sides of the ball, Kentucky only had about 60 or so scholarship players that first season. Indeed, only as the 1999 season approached was Mumme's program at the full complement of 85 scholarship players. Even so, 62 of them were freshmen, redshirt freshmen and sophomores.

More than his long-term mission to add talent and numbers, however, what Mumme quickly brought to the mix was a new attitude forged through the strength of his personality and rapport with his players.

"He's not just concerned with us as players," tight end James Whalen says. "It's almost like we're his children. He gets personal relationships going. He asks us about our families, our past. He's real interested in seeing us grow as people, as well as players. I think that's wonderful.

"And having him paired with Couch, that was perfect. Tim was frustrated. I think everyone was. And here comes this gunslinger from Texas and everyone's happy."

The gunslinger says he never had to chide the young gun.

"I can't think of a single time," Mumme says. "It was really amazing. But, you know, I look back over the quarterbacks we've had and I haven't had to get on any of them. That's why they're the quarterback. They're the kind of people who are going to do what's right."

When Tim Couch was named first-team All America in 1998, it continued what may be Mumme's most remarkable record. In his 10 seasons as a collegiate head coach, he's had four starting quarterbacks. All four were named to first-team All America lists. Dustin Dewald did it in the NAIA in 1991 when Mumme coached Iowa Wesleyan College. Chris Hatcher—current quarterbacks coach at Kentucky—did it twice (and was named national player of the year in Division II in 1994) at Valdosta State. Lance Funderburk followed Hatcher and likewise did it in 1996.

Perhaps most revealing is what Mumme did while still a high school coach in his native Texas. In 1988 he converted James Ritchey from center to quarterback. Ritchey went on from Copperas Cove High to play for Stephen F. Austin University, and he was a rookie with the Houston Oilers in 1996. Hal knows quarterbacks—even when they're not quarterbacks.

Fate brought them together—Mumme and Couch. But it was Mumme's history with quarterbacks that suggested the combination would revive Kentucky's football program and help propel Couch to stardom. They were kindred spirits.

"Oh yeah," Mumme affirms. "The thing I loved about Tim was that he was always real even-keeled. Whether he threw interceptions or threw touchdowns, he was the same guy. That was one of the fun things about coaching him, that he didn't get flustered."

Mumme would usually have running dialogues with Couch on the sidelines. But it wasn't always about football.

"I'd talk to him about hunting and fishing in Kentucky," Mumme says. "We'd talk about everything. Joke a lot. Back when we played Mississippi State last year and the weather was threatening a little bit, we joked about how that shouldn't give *him* problems—that it was kind of just like a spring day in Eastern Kentucky. The wind starts blowing through those hollers and everything, so it wouldn't be very hard to throw in this."

However, unlike Couch, who always dreamed and structured his life toward the goal of becoming a No. 1 draft pick, Mumme held no similar aspirations of loftiness. He never dreamed of coaching in Division I, let alone the pros.

"Nah," he says. "I didn't really care about getting to this level. I just liked coaching. I mean, it's obviously a lot better now. Financially it's better for my family and it's a lot more fun to have the media attention—all the stuff we get at this level—but it wasn't something I set out to do. I think when I graduated from Tarleton State (in history), my idea of the ideal job would be a high school coach in Texas for a long time, and if I did good at that maybe I'd get to be head coach at a small college."

The stars had other designs—and it led to an alliance that transformed the way a state regarded UK football. Couch and Mumme. County Cool and Parrothead Laid-Back. A natural. After all, once upon a time Jimmy Buffett, the Chief Parrothead himself, used to hang out in Nashville peddling country songs in obscurity.

Seamless it was, this pairing.

And yet, in the beginning of Mumme's tenure, there were players on Kentucky's team who cared little for Couch or Mumme. As the 1997 season approached, both of them had to win some hearts and minds.

6

The Air Raid Cranks Up

During one of the informal, non-supervised workouts that Kentucky's players would hold among themselves in the summer of 1997, Hal Mumme—who could watch but couldn't teach—began to hear a bombardment of angry expletives.

Tim Couch was grouped with several defensive players on a relay race team, but they were cursing at him, calling him everything they could think of. No banter here. Nothing playful about it. It was pointed and it was hostile.

"They just cussed him up one side and down the other," Mumme says, "and tried to really provoke him into fighting or quitting, one or the other. Tim just smiled back at them. He stayed out there, competed and went on."

When the workout ended, Mumme called Couch over as he walked nearby.

"I thought you handled that really well," Mumme told him. It was all that needed to be said.

Looking back on the incident, Mumme says: "They were going to test him—big time. A lot of the players were not Hal Mumme fans and they were not Tim Couch fans at first."

And when did that change? A grin crosses the coach's face.

"Oh, about two months later," he says, "after he'd thrown about seven touchdowns on 'em in one of our scrimmages. They were hugging him walking off the field after that."

The toughest challenge in Mumme's debut as coach and Couch's debut as the starting quarterback may well have been before the 1997 season began. It's never easy when a new coach comes in, of course. Understandably, many players feel a loyalty to the old coach who'd recruited them. Some also wonder if their position will be changed or if their playing status itself is in jeopardy.

In this case, there were other factors contributing to the tension. Curry had exuded something of a George Patton exterior, while Mumme was decidedly more Hawkeye Pierce. As a result, there were several players who, when it came right down to it, felt the stirrings of their Inner Frank Burns, blanching at the change. Did they want to be a part of this man's army? Worse, it wasn't going to be an army, anyway. It was going to be an air force with the new man's pretty boy throwing to his heart's content.

Which exposed yet another nerve. Many of those same players believed strongly in Billy Jack Haskins, who had demonstrated such courage and abandon, who had played with pain and played like he was one of them—another grunt, another dirt-smeared infantryman who'd do anything it took. And now what? They were supposed to be led by this young kid with all the clippings and the hype? Couch might as well have worn aviator glasses and a scarf to practice.

It didn't help that Mumme did things so differently. Curry, his chin set and his eyes hidden behind dark Ray-Bans, would hover over the practice area on a tower strategically located between two fields. The practices were tough and demanding, with lots of hitting. If you'd played for Vince Lombardi once upon a time, you tended to structure your practices that way.

But here was Mumme, sometimes scruffy and often wearing a sun visor or Panama hat to keep his longish, blondish hair out of his eyes. No general watching from a distance he, Mumme was right down there on the field, giving more hand signals from the sidelines than some major league third base coaches had done in their entire careers. A firm believer in not leaving his players' best efforts on the practice field, he also kept the workouts short. And there was virtually no contact. It was well organized, and full of repetitions, but there just wasn't the kind of hitting these players were used to. How were they going to be ready for Louisville, much less the SEC, with a regimen like this?

Not that some of the players were alone in their criticism. The good ol' boys around the SEC had never seen anything quite like it. It was like a picnic without fried chicken. It was like a rebel without a yell. Who was this Scarlett in a world full of Gables? Frankly, my dear, they didn't give a damn. It was all too ... too ... *dainty.*

Haskins, unwilling to accept a position change, had long since transferred to Division I-AA Delaware, where he had some success before another shoulder separation ended his career prematurely. So it was all on Couch—with one month in the spring to learn the offense and just a few weeks in August to polish its many nuances. He also had to ignore the cold shoulders (and sometimes colder comments) of some of his teammates.

"When I made the decision that Tim was the starter, we pretty much had a senior ball club that first year, particularly on defense," Mumme says. "And those guys were Billy Jack fans, not Tim Couch fans."

Billy Jack was appropriately named. He had the same noble, nothing-can-stop-me-when-the-cause-is-worth-it persona of the character Tom Laughlin made famous in a series of anti-establishment flicks in the 1970s. Talent had determined Mumme's choice, not heart—but that didn't make Billy Jack's demotion and subsequent self-imposed exile any easier to swallow by those who'd admired him. On the bloody morning after, one tin soldier had walked away. To them, *that* was the bottom line.

However, as the summer wore on and Couch began to excel in the two-a-days of August, many of them came around. Still, on the eve of Kentucky's season opener against Louisville, if the hostility had subsided, Mumme knew there was still skepticism to overcome. Many of the players weren't sure that his Air Raid would fly.

"When we played Louisville, there was only one guy on the field that day who knew we would win, and that was Tim Couch," Mumme says. "There were 10 other guys on offense *hoping* it would work, because they liked the way it practiced ..."

Mumme pauses, a wry smile forming.

"And there were 11 guys on defense who were pretty sure this shit *wasn't* gonna work."

They would find out otherwise. Quickly.

Until the series was renewed in 1994, Kentucky and Louisville hadn't played football against one another in 70 years. Kentucky won that initial renewal game in what would be Howard Schnellenberger's final season at U of L. But in the two years since, his successor, Ron Cooper, had beaten Kentucky each time. As the 1997 kickoff game neared, Cooper's team was a favorite to make it three in a row.

Cooper had gotten in some digs at Mumme's avoidance of hitting in pre-season practice, striking a sarcastic note to the chord of skepticism already pulsing in the media over Mumme's unorthodox ways. He probably felt even better when he stepped into Commonwealth Stadium on game day. Instead of the traditional "marching band" numbers blaring in the background while warmups were underway, Mumme had them playing Buffett tunes over the PA. If Mumme didn't know where he was gonna go when the volcano blow, Cooper and his Cards would be happy to provide the eruption and leave him the question to ponder in defeat.

Mumme came out relaxed and ready, even stopping to do a live interview as part of the pre-game coverage for one of the TV stations from Louisville. This was the man, after all, who, when asked by a local civic group when he was going to start throwing the football, had replied, "As soon as we get off the bus."

And so they did. In a first quarter that had Kentucky fans pinching themselves, Couch stunned Louisville with three touchdown passes—a 16-yarder to Lance Mickelsen, another 16-yarder to Jimmy Robinson and a 23-yard catch-and-run by Anthony White. Kentucky was throwing all kinds of formations at the confused U of L defense, receivers often springing wide open. Three times already the new Air Raid siren—surprising and delighting the crowd when it had sounded as UK first came onto the field—had sounded again to herald touchdowns. With 3:53 still left in the first quarter, it was 21-0, Wildcats.

"The guy who really felt it was going to go was Couch," Mumme says, reflecting back on that day. "He knew exactly what was going to work."

He smiles: "Of course, after the first quarter we had a bunch of guys start jumping on the bandwagon on the sidelines out there. It was pretty good. A pretty unique situation."

Louisville would regroup, fighting back with 17 unanswered points to draw within 21-17 when Chris Redman threw a 17-yard touchdown pass with 5:11 left in the third quarter. But Kentucky's next play from scrimmage sent a bold message about what life under Mumme and Couch would be about.

The ball was at the UK 20 when Couch took a short drop, turned and showed his remarkably quick release with a pass to Kio Sanford flanked in the right flat. Sanford took off, juking one defender near the line of scrimmage and leaping over another later in an 80-yard sprint to the goal line. As quick as that, Kentucky's lead was 28-17. As quick as that, Mumme's offense was bringing athletic talent to the fore that had been so submerged in the past that few even realized it was available.

Kentucky would win 38-24. More important, they had won with a demonstration of firepower so alien to the school's anemic offensive tradition, and so darn fun to watch, that it was hard to sense who was more enthralled, the players jumping around on the sidelines or the fans trading high fives and open mouths in the stands. The 38 points were the most scored by a Kentucky team in nine years.

The Air Raid was for real, and so was Couch. He'd completed 36 of 50 passes—four more completions than he'd had in the *entire season* of 1996—for 398 yards and four touchdowns. CNN/Sports Illustrated made him its national player of the week.

"It felt great," Couch said afterward, which was the football equivalent of a lotto winner saying they felt surprised. Beaming as he sat in front of rows of cameras, recorders and reporters, Couch was wearing a T-shirt with his flak jacket still loosely draped over his shoulders. The eye black applied before the game was hardly smudged. Now it was helping him deal with the glare of success that had suddenly re-entered his life.

Kentucky jumped to a 21-10 halftime lead the following week at Mississippi State and later rallied to claim a 27-22 advantage in the third period, but was outscored 13-0 in the final quarter and fell 35-27. It was a game Mumme thought had slipped through their fingers—indicative, perhaps, of a relatively young team that still hadn't learned how to win a tough SEC game on the road—but Couch did have another record-setting day by completing 39 passes in 64 attempts for 349 yards and four touchdowns. MSU coach Jackie Sherill, who coached Dan Marino at Pitt, had a different quarterback in mind when he was asked about Couch. "A young John Elway," he said.

While the loss was disappointing, the fireworks suggested UK's season opener had not been a fluke. The next week, at Indiana, proved it. Couch hit 24 of 32 passes and threw seven touchdowns in the game's first three quarters, sitting out the final 15 minutes as the Wildcats rolled, 49-7. It made Kentucky fans wonder. Big bad Florida was coming to Lexington. Might there be a chance? Was the unthinkable suddenly thinkable?

For Kentucky to have any chance against the Gators, the team that had thumped the Cats 65-0 a year before, there would have to be near flawless execution on offense with no turnovers. The worst thing that could have happened did. On UK's first play, Couch tried to get rid of the ball under a heavy rush and the ball was ruled an interception. Replays by CBS, which was televising the game nationally, clearly showed that the ball was on the ground before a Florida player got to it. Didn't matter, of course. The Gators had the ball at UK's 16 and scored on their first play on Fred Taylor's run. The floodgates opened. Florida jumped to a 28-0 first quarter lead.

Ironically, it was in the midst of this nightmare that Kentucky established that it was no longer shackled by its past. This was the kind of game that might have been 80-0 in previous years. It certainly seemed headed that way in the second quarter when Kentucky, again stymied and backed up in its own territory, lined up to punt. Instead, A.J. Simon took a short snap and threw to Whalen for a first down. The crowd went nuts. So did Kentucky's players, driving for a touchdown that took 10 plays and covered 94 yards. UK didn't allow Florida any points in the second quarter and trailed 28-7 at the break.

Florida was too much, of course, scoring 21 in the third period—but the fake punt had served to change Kentucky psychologically. Rather than roll over and play dead, the Wildcats would actually outscore the Gators over the final three periods, 28-27. It was a 55-28 loss, but perhaps something more important had been won.

The next week proved it. Alabama came to Lexington nationally ranked. But Kentucky, showing uncommon confidence, rallied from deficits on three occasions with much of the third quarter still to be played. Still, the memory of psychological whammies from the past loomed.

Many was the time UK had led a name team in Lexington only to lose in the closing seconds. It happened once against Florida, when Danny Weurfel threw a touchdown pass on the game's last play. And it had happened once against Alabama—back when Bill Curry was the Tide coach—the Tide winning on a touchdown pass at game's end, made all the worse when replay films showed one complete side of Bama's offensive line jump offside before the play with no flag thrown.

So on this night, when Couch threw touchdown passes to White and Kevin Coleman to vault Kentucky from a 17-13 deficit to a 27-17 lead with 5:15 left in the third quarter, fans had to wonder: Would the black cloud descend again? Would Kentucky, playing so well, trip into the abyss once more?

Sure enough, the game took an ominous turn. Bama scored two touchdowns in a five-minute span to jump ahead, 31-27, and continued to maintain momentum, lining up for a field goal to pad their lead with about seven minutes to play. But as Brian Cunningham kicked the ball, Kentucky's David Ginn, a walk-on, jumped high near the line of scrimmage and blocked it. The ball soared high into the air and directly into the hands of Anwar Stewart, who ran 68 yards for a touchdown. Suddenly, a game slipping away had turned into a 34-31 lead.

Still, the game wasn't Kentucky's. Cunningham kicked a 37-yard field goal with only four seconds to play to force an overtime. Even so, a different feeling seemed to course through the crowd. Where resignation to a heartbreaking loss had dominated before, there was instead a sense of possibility. Maybe it was the stars. Maybe it was the brilliance of Couch. Whatever the reason, things didn't seem the same. For a change, a sense of excitement trumped a sense of dread.

Alabama got the ball first, but its drive ended when Tremayne Martin made a huge hit to force a fumble that Jeremy Bowie recovered. Kentucky's offense took over but bogged down and faced third-and-11 at the Tide 36. Mumme was faced with a decision.

"Tim came over as he always does during the timeouts and Craig (Yeast) came over, too," Mumme remembers. "Craig insisted he could beat his guy on a curl route."

Back to the line of scrimmage they came, hoping at least to get close enough for a game-winning field goal attempt. Yeast sprinted downfield and then cut inside, turning for the ball. Couch drilled it into his arms. Showing his uncanny ability to blur by tacklers, Yeast shot like a cannon past an Alabama defensive back and was into the end zone in an instant.

It had happened.

It had really happened.

Kentucky 40, Alabama 34.

Still cheering, most people didn't move at first. Elbert Couch was not among them. He'd already jumped out of the stands and ran to find his son. When he looked around, he saw his 72-year-old father standing beside him. "How'd you get down here?" Elbert said. "Well," his father said. "I just jumped down that wall like you did."

They were jumping everywhere. Fans began to pour onto the field, running up to the celebrating players, running wherever their emotion led them. It was a strange feeling, a heady mix of the dazed and the enthused. It wasn't the ugly kind of crowd you sometimes see in situations like this. It was as if this moment was so new to them, so deliciously rare, that they were running rampant around it and yet pausing to stop and savor it at the same time. When UK's players took a knee at midfield for a short prayer, many a fan beside them bowed their heads as well.

Never had the goalposts come down in Commonwealth Stadium, but they did on this night. C.M. Newton wisely told police and officials to let the fans at the posts. "If I wasn't so old," Newton later would say, "I'd have joined them."

Those left in the stands weren't about to leave. They stood and watched it all unfold. How many years had they waited for a night like this? In the end zone bleachers, the band was playing the old Bruce Chanel song from the early 1960s: "*Heyyyyyy, hey-hey baby! I wanna know woah woah, if you'll be my girl.*" Teenagers and fortysomethings began singing along. Little old ladies traded high fives. Some people just stood on their seats, smiling and shaking their heads slowly at the sheer joy of it all.

It would matter little that Alabama, its confidence perhaps shattered that night, would wind up with a losing record. What mattered was that Kentucky had banished, once and for all, the specter of certain calamity. You'd always lose your share of close ones, of course, but suddenly there was no longer the sense of inevitability to losing the big one.

Kentucky football had turned a corner.

Couch had again been his prolific self. He hit 32 of 49 passes for 355 yards and four touchdowns. He'd also been intercepted three times, but who was counting? *The New York Daily News* named Couch its national player of the week.

With a defense that struggled most of the time, Kentucky wasn't assured of anything, of course—and the quirkiness of a team in a new system would be reflected through the rest of the season. UK blew a 14-0 first quarter lead at South Carolina and fell 38-24, then destroyed Northeast Louisiana at home, 49-14. In a game played mostly in the rain, Kentucky lost to Georgia in Athens, 23-13, but had shown it could compete by outgaining the Bulldogs in total yardage, 436-275. Kentucky led LSU 21-20 at halftime in Lexington, but its defense weakened in the second half under LSU's punishing ground game and the Cats fell 63-28. A 21-10 win at Vandy gave UK a 5-5 record, and at least raised the possibility of a bowl bid as a home game with Tennessee awaited.

It figured to be fun, regardless. The game would match Couch against Peyton Manning, and a record Commonwealth Stadium crowd of 61,076 came to see it.

What they had no way of knowing at the time, of course, was that they were watching the two players who would go No. 1 in the NFL draft over the next two years.

What they left with that day, however, was the certain knowledge that they might never again see a duel like the one Couch and Manning put on.

Together they combined for 999 yards passing. Couch hit 35 of 50 passes for 476 yards and two touchdowns. Manning completed 25 of 35 for 523 yards and five touchdowns. In all, the two teams amassed 1,329 total yards. Trailing only 24-21 at halftime, Kentucky would wither and lose, 59-31. If there was disappointment, it was tempered by the surprising success this team had fashioned. But more than that, there was an anticipation that the best was yet to come. Passion was suddenly compatible with Kentucky football.

Never had that been more evident than in the second quarter—when Kio Sanford turned a short pass from Couch into a twisting, tackle-breaking, leaping, zig-zag 87-yard touchdown. ESPN nominated it for its "outstanding college football play of the year" ESPY award. And when you watched it again on tape—as countless Kentuckians did countless times—you could see another element to the passion of Sanford's run.

Onto the screen a figure appeared, running like crazy, trying to throw a block maybe 60 yards downfield. It was Couch, of course.

And it was the best darn 5-6 season a fellow could have imagined.

Couch hadn't fully mastered the offense, but you'd hardly know it. Three touchdowns in the first quarter of the first game, and now a slew of school records—single game and season—had fallen. How had Couch gotten out of the gate so quickly and smoothly? Talent explains a lot of it, of course, but James Whalen cites another factor: Matt Mumme, the coach's son and Couch's backup.

"He'd been running this offense since the fifth grade," Whalen points out. "Any question Tim had, he didn't have to write it down or wait for Coach to come around. Matt was there every day to answer them. He'd tell Tim, 'This is your read, this is what you need to do here, this is the guy's route, here's how many steps, release it in this many seconds.' Matt probably knew the offense as well as Coach Mumme."

Couch, of course, was quick to learn. And quick to embrace the offense.

Hal Mumme reflects: "The surprising thing about that first year was that Tim did a great job of getting the receiver corps to buy into the system early on. Guys like Kevin Coleman and Kio Sanford, Yeast and Mikelsen ... they were skeptical. They were *very* skeptical. I think they'd heard how they were going to throw the ball before in their careers, and it never happened. But Tim did a good job convincing them that, 'Hey, if we just do what he's saying and do it right, it'll work.' "

Couch had completed only his sophomore season, and already it was clear that he'd be a Heisman front-runner the following year. More talent was coming in. Yeast would be back, too, and the defense could only get better. If they could do this much in the first season of Mumme's system, what goodies were still in store?

They were not the thoughts a Kentucky football fan usually had at season's end. Heismans? Bowls? Air raid sirens and touchdowns galore?

It all led to the rarest of questions:

"Hey, when does spring practice start?"

7

Almost Heaven

Throughout the spring and summer leading to the 1998 season, Kentucky's players wore tee shirts with "1-1-99" plastered on them. The legend on the shirts reflected the goal in their hearts: a bowl appearance on New Year's Day. Cynics might have scoffed at such pretense, suggesting the shirts should read "0-4-47" instead—the last number indicating how many years UK had been an "oh-fer" in January bowl appearances.

Cynicism, of course, doesn't win football games—and not a trace of it lurked as the 1998 season approached. Buoyed by the surprising success and offensive firepower of 1997 and confident that Couch would show even greater mastery of Mumme's offense with a year's experience behind him, Kentucky set its sights high.

Nothing in the spring game diminished those hopes. The defense gave every indication that, while not formidable, it would show significant improvement. Couch, meanwhile, was Couch. Against second-stringers in the Blue-White game, he threw for 316 yards and four touchdowns—in one quarter. By the time the annual rivalry game with Louisville rolled around to kick off the season, Kentucky's players exhibited a confidence and sense of mission uncommon at a school where high-flying football fantasies rarely touched down.

Kentucky had not won a season opener on the road in 12 years, but Couch and his teammates wasted little time establishing their intent to make 1998 something special. In a new stadium in a new season on what Louisville figured would be a new day, the same old story played out. Just as he'd shocked the Cardinals with a trio of first-quarter touchdown passes in 1997, Couch shattered them with five first-half TD throws this time—including three in the second quarter that propelled Kentucky to a 41-10 halftime lead.

When he left the game early in the fourth quarter with Kentucky leading 61-16, Couch had a truckload of gaudy stats: 29 of 39 passing for 498 yards, seven touchdowns and zero interceptions. In U of L's inaugural game in Papa John's Stadium—where an inordinate number of blue-clad spectators populated the stands (many had purchased Louisville season tickets just to have a seat for this one)—Kentucky won, 68-34.

Simply unable to keep up with the speed and savvy of receivers who often broke wide open in underneath routes, Louisville mostly watched helplessly as 14 UK players caught passes and six of them caught passes for touchdowns. Yeast, per usual, was the leader with nine receptions for 150 yards and two touchdowns.

Most of the time, Couch had all day to throw—and when he didn't, he was sidestepping the rush and still delivering, the most notable instance coming in the second quarter when tight end Jimmy Haley extended into the air at the goal line and reached up and back to make a one-handed grab that put Kentucky up, 31-10. CNN made the catch its "Play of the Day."

Kentucky set school records for total offense (801 yards), passing yardage (571), first downs (37) and passing first downs (24). And when backup Matt Mumme also threw for a touchdown, UK tied its own SEC record for passing touchdowns with eight. The 68 points were the most a Kentucky team had scored in 47 years.

When Kentucky opened its home schedule the following week against Eastern Kentucky, further evidence that football was not the same in Lexington was forthcoming. Kentucky won 52-7, but coaches, players and fans alike fretted over the way the Wildcats had performed—particularly in the third quarter when they settled for a touchdown and field goal and also yielded their only touchdown to EKU. When was the last time a Kentucky observer could view a 45-point win and feel flat about it? Never.

"It's the worst run blocking game since I've been here," a disgusted Mumme said. "There were a lot of missed assignments." It showed. For instance, Derek Homer, who had rushed 19 times for123 yards in the opener, carried 16 times against Eastern for a meager 58 yards.

Couch, however, was still on a roll. He had five touchdown passes, tying him with Babe Parilli for the school record for career TD throws with 50. Two games into the season, he was 61 of 80 passing for 870 yards and 12 touchdowns. He had not thrown an interception.

All that would change against Indiana—the worst game in Couch's career under Mumme. Deciding to use a "soft" zone defense that allowed them to hone in on UK's underneath routes while also discouraging the bomb, the Hoosiers rushed only four linemen and tried to cut off every passing avenue.

It worked. Kentucky had six turnovers in all, and Couch had two-thirds of them by throwing four interceptions. The dependable Yeast was in a funk as well. On the third play of the game, Yeast was wide open but dropped an easy catch. Two plays later he dropped another. It was an omen. Mumme would later review the film and say that out of 79 offensive plays, Kentucky made major errors in 24 of them. Bad throws, missed blocks, fumbles, penalties ... all of it was threatening to eliminate the giddiness of Kentucky's 2-0 start.

Kentucky trailed 20-3 in the final minute of the first half when Mumme underscored his gambling nature—and the somber reality of a game turned ominous—by electing a fourth-down run from the Indiana 2 rather than kicking a field goal. Homer scored, barely, with just seven seconds remaining to make it 20-10. Surely that would be the turning point. Surely Couch would crank things up in the second half.

Instead, things got darker. Early in the third quarter, Indiana took a 27-10 lead when a bad center snap by Jason Watts sailed over the punter's head and was recovered by IU's Aaron Williams in the end zone. And still, Couch couldn't get untracked. With less than six minutes remaining in the third quarter, UK remained down 17 and was facing fourth-and-21 from its 21-yard line.

Anyone well versed in the history of Kentucky football could have told you what normally would have happened next. A shanked punt. Or another wayward snap. Or a decent punt—only to be followed by a touchdown-yielding lapse by a defense that had been on the field too long. And, of course, a loss.

What happened instead was Parrothead stuff.

Per his father's instructions, Matt Mumme, lined up as a blocking back in punt formation, took the short snap and floated a pass to Garry Davis, who'd blown past his defender by a step or two near the left sideline. Davis made the catch and raced the final 60 yards or so to the end zone. The 79-yard play cut the deficit to 27-17.

Kentucky's defense had bottled up Indiana's quick and elusive quarterback, Antwaan Randle-El, all day (he completed only 12 of 34 passes and rushed for only five yards on 16 carries). But now it needed to do more. Enthused by the success of Mumme's gamble, they produced.

Early in the fourth quarter, freshman safety David Johnson forced a fumble that tackle George Massey recovered. Two plays later, Couch came alive, hitting Anthony White for a 48-yard touchdown pass to make it 27-24. On Indiana's next possession, Dennis Johnson and Marlon McCree smothered Randle-El as he attempted a shovel pass, the ball landing in the hands of UK linebacker John Rader, who ran 46 yards for a touchdown. Kentucky was suddenly up 31-27, and that's how it ended.

Couch did complete 38 of 53 passes for 301 yards, but the numbers didn't reflect the numbness of his performance. Mumme, however, notes that even on an off day, Couch did not withdraw into a shell.

"The great thing about Tim is that he doesn't rattle," Mumme says. "It was the same to him when he threw an interception as when he threw a touchdown pass. I'd probably say that the Indiana game was his worst. He and Yeast both had a bad day. But if you watch the highlights film, you'll see Tim in there, cheering everybody on and talking about how they can't beat us. He was really struggling in his own game, but he was still picking everybody up.

"You know, nobody ever thought we'd lose that game. Even though we were down, everybody knew somebody was going to make a play. And Tim was right in the mix of that."

It was encouraging that Kentucky could win on an off day by Couch—a win in large part accomplished by its defense, which was still thin in depth and lacking in size but improved in speed, primarily because of position changes made in the spring.

Kentucky was 3-0—its best start in 14 years—but next up was Florida in The Swamp. The Gators ripped apart Kentucky's secondary, gaining 452 yards and scoring six touchdowns through the air in a 51-35 win. Going in, UK's players believed they had a legitimate shot at an upset. For awhile, it appeared possible. That it didn't materialize doesn't detract, however, from extraordinary performances by Couch and Yeast—particularly Yeast.

Small, speedy and owner of an almost surrealistic ability to slip slide away from would-be tacklers in the secondary, Yeast silenced the Florida crowd with a 100-yard kickoff return (it actually was closer to 105 yards), a 97-yard touchdown reception and a 74-yard touchdown reception. He finished with 331 all-purpose yards and caught six passes for a school-record 206 yards, his 34.3 yards per catch average another school mark.

Couch was 40 of 61 for 406 yards and three touchdowns. He was intercepted twice. The scoring punch Kentucky displayed was no doubt a factor when Bob Stoops, then Florida's defensive coordinator, decided to hire UK assistant Mike Leach as his offensive coordinator after Stoops was named head coach at Oklahoma at season's end.

Yeast's 100-yard return had come on UK's first possession to forge a 7-7 tie. And his 97-yard scoring reception gave Kentucky a 14-7 lead—Couch throwing from the end zone and Yeast catching it on the run at about the Florida 25. A Florida defensive back lunged and grabbed at him, but the slippery Yeast darted out of his grasp in an instant and soon was jogging, then walking, into the end zone.

"It was a called play," Yeast says. "They were trying to play me bump and run. At the time, I didn't think anybody could play me that way. We'd had the same thing happen against them the previous year with Kio Sanford, but Kio dropped the ball. I just made sure that I wasn't going to drop it."

Indeed, when Couch was a sophomore playing the Gators in Commonwealth Stadium, he'd dropped back into the end zone and thrown to a streaking Sanford up the middle. Sanford, who had a few steps on the Gator secondary, had it sail just off his fingertips. It would have been a remarkable catch, to be sure, but it was within a hair's length of succeeding. The play would have gone 98 yards.

The game in Gainesville likewise produced a missed opportunity. Halfway into the second quarter, with the score tied at 14, Kentucky appeared to have a sure touchdown as Couch threw a perfect pass to an open Quentin McCord. But McCord inexplicably let the ball drop between his arms near the goal line. After that, Florida scored three touchdowns in a shockingly short span of 2:22 and the game was sealed.

Still, Couch later hooked up with Yeast for a 74-yard touchdown—a pass that James Whalen, the tight end, says is the most memorable Couch pass he ever witnessed.

"He was getting hit one way and getting hit another way, and he threw just a rocket right to Craig on a little curl route, and then Craig took off," Whalen says. "And Tim's body, when he threw it? His feet are horizontal this way, his shoulders are horizontal the other way, and he's still throwing a frozen rope."

If losing at Florida was a foregone conclusion to most observers, playing at Arkansas the next week was regarded as the first critical challenge to Kentucky's bowl aspirations. The Razorbacks were revived under rookie coach Houston Nutt. Formerly the head man at Murray State, Nutt had backers who lobbied Newton to hire him during Kentucky's coaching search. Even Arkansas athletic director Frank Broyles, who wasn't looking for a coach at the time, had put in a word for Nutt. As it turned out, of course, Nutt wound up at Arkansas and had a great rookie campaign. Arkansas would later take national champion Tennessee to the wire in a loss in Knoxville, and the Razorbacks would also earn a bid to the Citrus Bowl.

Facing a ranked team on the road for the second straight week, Kentucky and Couch appeared unstoppable early on. With touchdown passes to Yeast, McCord and Lance Mickelsen in each of the first three periods, Couch led UK to a 20-7 advantage. Then the wheels came off.

After kicking a pair of third quarter field goals to cut the margin to 20-13, Arkansas rallied for a pair of touchdowns in the fourth quarter. The game turned when Couch was intercepted on a pass intended for Yeast. Had Yeast come back toward the ball, the worst that could have happened was that the pass would have been broken up. Yeast had made such a move countless times on similar pass routes in the past, but this time he stood flat-footed. The interception set up the first of two Arkansas touchdowns in the fourth quarter that lifted the Razorbacks out of a seven-point deficit and into a 27-20 lead.

After the game, Mumme said the interception was Yeast's fault, then shifted the blame to himself, saying he'd called for a pass designed against man-to-man defenses when Arkansas was in a zone. Then Couch weighed in, saying it was first miscommunication between him and the coach, then between him and Yeast. "But he was still open," Couch said. "I just threw it late. That one play changed the game."

Asked about that play in the summer of 1999, Yeast confirmed what some had long suspected. It was no secret that he'd cramped up so badly in his legs that he missed most of the fourth quarter—including UK's final, desperation drive that ended on the game's last play, when Couch's pass from inside the Arkansas 10 into the end zone was a shade too high and behind his intended receiver. But had Yeast cramped up earlier in the quarter, when the interception came?

"Yes, I was cramping up even then," Yeast says. "I was out there when maybe I shouldn't have been. But, you know, things happen. I was cramping, but I was still trying to go at the same time because that's my nature."

Nobody blamed Couch for the missed touchdown pass on the game's final play. He'd had to throw the ball a tad too high to get it over the raised arms of an Arkansas linebacker who'd dropped to clog the passing lane a few yards up from the goal line. Not that it was much consolation. Kentucky had played hard against two strong teams on the road in consecutive weeks and had nothing to show for it. The Wildcats were 3-2. Walking off the field, Tim Couch was in tears.

"I was walking back to the locker room with him," Rena Vicini says, "and everybody was yelling, 'Tim Couch!'—asking him for his autograph. And he's sobbing so hard he can't hardly walk. It just devastated him."

He would recover quickly. He was the same matter-of-fact Couch after he'd composed himself in the locker room and was ushered into the area where the media waited. It was, however, gut-check time for both him and the team. All that talk of 1-1-99 likely meant nothing now. Without a revival, and fast, any bowl—let alone one on New Year's Day—would elude them.

In the next two weeks, the revival was complete.

First came a home win over South Carolina, 33-28. Seeking to re-establish a decent running game, Mumme kept the ball on the ground early. Couch attempted only four passes in the first quarter, completing two for 13 yards. But the running game was clicking. Anthony White—a back who catches the ball as well as he runs with it—gained 108 rushing yards on 18 carries and 117 passing yards on eight catches. Couch, meanwhile, would keep his string of 300-yard passing games alive, going 29 of 42 for 315 yards and three touchdowns.

Then came the turning point, LSU in Baton Rouge. It would be Kentucky's third road game in four weeks—all against ranked opponents. The night before the game, *deja vu* visited Mumme and Couch. "We had the same feeling that we'd had before the Alabama game," Mumme says. "We felt we were going to win.

Win they did, shocking the rowdy LSU crowd by pulling an end-around play on third-and-12 from their 24-yard line with only a minute to play and the score tied. McCord darted around from his wideout slot on the right as Couch faked a handoff up the middle and planted the ball on his hip, a perfect fake. McCord took it, continued around left end, cut up and then across the field for a 38-yard gain to the LSU 38. After Couch hit tight end Haley on a 14-yard out pattern that UK had not run all night, Seth Hanson came in to kick a 33-yard field goal as time expired. UK won, 39-36.

The reverse was a golden moment in the annals of chicanery. Kentucky had seemed content to run out the clock and take their chances in overtime—twice running plays up the middle that netted a minus two yards. Had Mumme, the quintessential go-for-it guy, turned timid in the warm Louisiana night? Even some UK players were wondering.

"There was a feeling of 'Why are we doing this? Are we playing into their hands?' " Whalen says. "I don't know if Coach Mumme had the thought of putting that in earlier. I think it just kinda hit him after the first two plays.

"After the first two plays, I think that even everyone on *our* sideline thought we were going into overtime. We figured, well, we've come this far, we didn't want to throw an interception or shoot ourselves in the foot. We were just going to play smart football. And then Coach comes up with just a wonderful call."

"Well," says Mumme, "we had talked about running that thing for most of the fourth quarter, maybe even some of the third quarter. I remember ol' Jonas Liening, our left tackle, coming over and telling me he thought it was there. You know, when the left tackle can call it, it's pretty obvious.

"But for some reason, we just didn't run it until we got the ball at the end. We were up by two touchdowns for awhile there and we really didn't need it. Then all of a sudden we were tied up, and it just seemed like the natural course of things."

Had Mumme decided on trying the play before the first two runs up the middle? Or was it an impromptu decision during the timeout—a timeout called not by Kentucky but by LSU?

"No, we knew," Mumme says. "I knew we'd try to do it right there. We'd kinda set it up with the two running plays. We were hoping they'd bite in there pretty hard."

Suddenly, Mumme's face takes on a Buffett-like aura.

"Actually," he says, "what I was hoping was that we could just run the ball down the field on 'em for a touchdown. When I called the two running plays? The first choice was to knock all the LSU guys down and for Anthony White or Derek Homer just to run down the field a long ways. But LSU wouldn't go along with that, so we had the reverse ready."

With that, he grins like a Cheshire cat.

What really went on during that timeout? James Whalen remembers Mumme's words: "He says, 'Boys, let's try somethin'. I don't know if it'll work. We might have to go into overtime, but let's just try something and see what happens.' "

TIM COUCH AND JENNIFER ADAMS WERE VOTED MOST POPULAR DURING THEIR SENIOR YEAR IN HIGH SCHOOL.

Photo Courtesy of Leslie County High School

COACH BEDER AND TIM COUCH AT PRACTICE.

Photo Courtesy of Leslie County High School

TIM COUCH WAS
ELECTED ONE OF
KENTUCKY'S TOP 15
SENIORS
COMBINATION
PLAYERS; REGION 14,
1ST TEAM WING.

Photo Courtesy of Leslie County
High School

Photo Courtesy of Leslie County High School

TIM COUCH, PICTURED WITH HIS PARENTS, WAS
CHOSEN KENTUCKY PLAYER OF THE YEAR BOTH IN
1994 AND 1995, AS WELL AS MR. FOOTBALL AND
WAS THE FIRST MALE KENTUCKIAN TO RECEIVE
THESE NATIONAL HONORS.

TIM COUCH AND
PAUL HORNUNG
AT THE HIGH
SCHOOL
FOOTBALL
AWARDS
BANQUET.

Photo Courtesy of Leslie
County High School

Photo Courtesy of Mollie B. Sizemore

TIM COUCH (2) WAS QUARTERBACK FOR LESLIE
COUNTY HIGH SCHOOL, HERE SHOWN IN THE FIRST
ROUND PLAYOFFS AT CARDINAL STADIUM,
LOUISVILLE, KENTUCKY VS KNOX CENTRAL.

Photo Courtesy of Mollie B. Sizemore

TIM COUCH RECEIVING GATORADE CIRCLE OF
CHAMPION AWARD FOR FOUR NATIONAL RECORDS
AND PLAYER OF THE YEAR.

Photo Credit: Brian Spurlock

TIM COUCH ENDED HIS KENTUCKY CAREER WITH 8,435 PASSING YARDS AND 74 TOUCHDOWN PASSES.

Photo Credit: Brian Spurlock

IN THE OUTBACK BOWL AGAINST PENN STATE, ON JANUARY 1, 1999, TIM COUCH COMPLETED 30 OF 48 PASS ATTEMPTS FOR 366 YARDS AND TWO TOUCHDOWNS.

IN KENTUCKY'S 55-17 VICTORY OVER VANDERBILT, TIM COUCH BROKE SEC SINGLE-SEASON RECORDS FOR TOTAL OFFENSE, PASSING YARDAGE AND PASS COMPLETIONS.

Photo Credit: Brian Spurlock

Photo Credit: Brian Spurlock

TIM COUCH AND COACH HAL MUMME LED KENTUCKY TO A 7-4 REGULAR-SEASON RECORD IN 1998, THE TEAM'S FIRST WINNING RECORD IN NINE YEARS.

TIM COUCH GOT THIS PASS OFF EVEN WITH JACKSONVILLE JAGUARS TACKLE SETH PAYNE AT HIS FEET.

UNFORTUNATELY, TIM DIDN'T GET AWAY FROM THE BALTIMORE RAVENS' MICHAEL McCRARY THIS TIME.

McCord also recalls what Mumme told him: "He asked me, 'Can you get the reverse?' since I'd gotten it the week before (an 80-yard touchdown run against South Carolina). I told him I thought I could. But he said, 'If anything works out bad, just fall. Don't fumble, don't turn the ball over.'"

As Couch called the play in the huddle, he looked at McCord.

"Quentin, we need this," Couch said.

Says McCord: "I didn't want to let the team down, or him."

The fake handoff was a thing of beauty, so well done that the ESPN2 camera followed the gaggle of helmets and bodies converging in the middle as Couch looked straight ahead and kept the ball tucked on his hip for McCord to take. "Tim is probably the best person I've ever seen with play fakes," Whalen says. "No one really knew where the ball was until about 10 yards up the field, when you see Quentin racing up that sideline."

In typical fashion, Couch was also racing—far up the right side of the field, looking to block somebody as McCord angled his way back toward Couch. "He told me after the game that if I'd just hesitated a bit, I could have gone for a touchdown," McCord says. "You see a quarterback wanting to make a play like that and you figure, gosh, if he wants to win that badly, I need to win as badly as he does."

Throughout the momentous game, Couch had demonstrated just how badly he wanted it. Kentucky scored on its first possession "and that," Whalen says, "was the key. You could just see it in Tim's eyes, like 'Boys, we're not going to lose this game.' And we followed him, basically, the whole way. Rode him like a horse."

The horse was a thoroughbred. Twice on touchdown passes to Yeast, Couch put the ball in trajectories that few men can. They were bullet passes, and yet they were touch passes. Each throw had no room for error, catching Yeast each time just before he flew out the side of the end zone— one of the passes in particular a gem, the ball eluding by inches the fingertips of an LSU defensive back who was in perfect position but came up with nothing but air.

Couch passed for 391 yards and three touchdowns, Whalen catching the other one. Kentucky was 5-2 and alive again. But in the Southeastern Conference, luxury is a fleeting thing. There was no time to sit back and savor. Next up was 11th-ranked Georgia in Lexington.

If Arkansas was a heartbreaker, Georgia was—or so it seemed at the time—a backbreaker. Despite jumping all over the Bulldogs from the outset (UK led 10-0 after one quarter), despite finishing with a huge statistical advantage in virtually every category (including 530-332 yards in total offense), Kentucky lost 28-26. Seth Hanson had a chance to win it with a 49-yard field goal on the game's last play, but a bad snap bounced off holder Matt Mumme's arm.

Couch passed for 326 yards, but his naked bootleg on fourth down from the Georgia 1 in the first quarter, when UK was trying to increase its lead to 17-0, was sniffed out by linebacker Orantes Grant, who tackled Couch for a loss of three. Ironic it was that in defeat, Kentucky had played perhaps its best overall game. The defense caused one fumble, had an interception and four sacks. It held Georgia to 185 yards rushing and just 147 through the air.

Kentucky, however, had only a 5-3 record to show for it. Mississippi State, which would go on to win the SEC West, was coming into Lexington next. It was moment-of-truth time again—and again UK responded. So did Couch, who saved perhaps the most magical moment of his career to produce the game-winning touchdown.

Kentucky had gone five years without a bowl. It needed a sixth win to qualify. In addition, whatever slim chance of still making a New Year's Day game made a win over Mississippi State essential.

It was a war from the start. Twice UK came back from deficits in the first half, but still trailed, 22-18, at the break. By the midpoint of the third quarter, Kentucky had fallen behind by 11 at 29-18. Ominous, too, was the fact that Couch had suffered a sprained thumb in the first quarter. That, and a clever Mississippi State defensive scheme that virtually eliminated Kentucky's effectiveness with its short, slipstream screen passes to wideouts, made the situation appear all the more bleak.

In the gloom, however, Couch began to fashion one of his most memorable performances. Attacking the defense by focusing on seams left open in the middle, he led Kentucky on scoring drives of 48, 72 and 87 yards—the last touchdown, the one with magic written all over it, catapulting the Cats to a 37-29 lead.

It was a six-yard pass from Couch to Yeast, and it was the stuff of legend. As Couch dropped back to throw, Mississippi State tore through Kentucky's linemen and converged on the quarterback with alarming quickness. Backpedaling, bumped and beginning to fall backwards near the 15-yard line, Couch somehow got rid of the ball.

But no, it was more than that. He had seen Yeast, streaking from right to left near the back of the end zone with three MSU players on his heels. As he was falling backwards, Couch launched the ball on a looping, languid trajectory that led Yeast perfectly. Jumping between strides as the ball finally made its descent, Yeast grabbed it—his body shielding the ball from the defenders hot on his trail. On his back, Couch witnessed it. On their feet, the Kentucky crowd pinched themselves, then erupted in cheers.

"It was one of those touchdowns that you just pull out of a bag," said Mississippi State coach Jackie Sherrill in the aftermath. "Craig Yeast made that play. We had Couch sacked."

Well, that was the point, wasn't it? Couch *was* sacked. And yet, he'd made the play. There was no mistaking that his pass was not simply a desperation lob with luck plastered all over it. No, he'd led Yeast with the throw—had led him perfectly. No accident here.

"No, hell no," Rena Vicini says. "Nothing was an accident with him."

"It was one of the greatest plays I've ever seen," Mumme says. "I can't think of any better."

It not only gave Kentucky a 37-29 lead, it also proved to be the game-winner. Mississippi drew within 37-35 with only 3:31 to play when Wayne Madkin hooked up with Kevin Prentiss for a 43-yard touchdown pass, but when the Bulldogs tried to tie the game on a two-point conversion run, UK defensive tackle Mark Jacobs stopped Madkin for a loss. Then Couch engineered a drive to kill the clock.

Kentucky was 6-3. More significant, Kentucky was bowl eligible. Had they reflected on just how close they'd come to beating Arkansas and Georgia, how 8-1 had been almost a reality, they would have seen the fine line between a very good season and a great one. They were two narrow defeats away from greatness. It was almost heaven.

Such speculation, however, is the province of pundits, not players. Nothing could diminish the significance of this victory—not given Kentucky's history. Likewise, nothing could dim the expectation of what still could be accomplished.

As a way to keep the focus on each week's mission, Mumme had banned the players from wearing the 1-1-99 tee shirts once the season began. But as he stood in the jubilant locker room, he peeled off his sweatshirt and sweater to reveal the 1-1-99 shirt he'd secretly donned before the game. Amidst the cheers and laughter, tears flowed. "We've got guys with big old tears in their eyes," defensive coordinator Mike Major told Janet Graham of the *Cincinnati Post*.

Under the grandstands, Rena Vicini, who always went there in a game's final minutes to take care of details for the post-game press conference, was crying as well. Understand that Vicini, who grew up just down the road from Hyden in Lynch, Ky., wept because she is a fan as much as she is a UK administrator, wept because of her Eastern Kentucky heritage and the player it had produced.

The Wildcat Den where Hal Mumme conducts the press conference from a podium is just down from the UK locker room. Vicini waited in the hallway to make certain Couch wasn't just interviewed on the fly, but could sit at the podium. Mumme finished up, but still no Couch.

"I started getting frustrated," Vicini says, "and I got someone on the walkie talkie and said 'Get Tim out here right now.' And he says, "I'm trying to, but they're celebrating and everything.' Finally, I heard them say, 'He's on his way.' "

Moments later, Couch appeared in the hallway.

"As soon as I looked at him, I started crying," Vicini says. "I said, 'You *know* what, Tim. You know where I'm from and I know where you're from.' And he started crying, too."

She showed him a ring on her finger. It was from the 1993 Peach Bowl.

"I'm not wearing my national championship basketball ring, am I?" she said to Couch, showing him the bowl ring. "This is what makes my heart pound. Thank you, Tim."

They hugged.

"Here I'd been trying to rush him to the press conference," Vicini says, chuckling at the memory, "and now we're standing out there in the hallway, cryin' and huggin'."

"We're going to a bowl," Vicini said, savoring each word.

"We're goin', we're goin'," said Couch.

Tears of joy.

A week later, Tim Couch would weep again. This time they wouldn't be tears of joy.

8

Triumph and Tragedy

November 14, 1998—Senior Day in Commonwealth Stadium. As always, the pre-game pageantry focused on Kentucky's seniors. Each player was introduced over the PA system, each gliding across the field to cheers and meeting his parents at midfield with a handshake and a hug.

The day was cold and gray, as if nature itself was confirming the finality of things. Long gone was the brilliant sunshine and summer swelter when UK had opened its season with rousing success. Fading fast was the cool crispness of fall, when the team had rallied to become bowl eligible.

They stood on the field, alone with their parents and their thoughts. If they reflected on their careers, they could see how far they'd come from the disappointment of the early years—all of it made irrelevant by a season still alive with promise.

Among them was Jason Watts, the center, the heart of the offensive line, the player who was making his thirty-third consecutive start, the player who'd suffered a concussion and missed the second half of the Arkansas game only to be back in the lineup the following week. His parents had come from Florida for this moment, made all the more poignant as the band began playing "My Old Kentucky Home." The crowd, as always, sang along.

"By and by hard times come a-knocking at the door ... "

There was no way to know, of course; no way to foresee how those words would prove prophetic less than 24 hours later when the awful news arrived. Artie Steinmetz, who had transferred from Michigan State to play for his home state, and Scott Brock, the best friend of Tim Couch since childhood, had been killed.

They were riding in a pickup driven by Watts, who'd lost control and swerved, the truck leaving the road, hitting a berm and flipping twice end over end. All three men were thrown from the truck. When the accident happened, at 6:58 a.m. that Sunday, they were only a few miles from a farm where they'd planned to go deer hunting, some 70 miles south of Lexington. Watts, in hysterics, one of his arms torn open, ran back and forth to Brock and Steinmetz, pleading with them to stay alive. There was no response.

"They hunt no more for the 'possum and the coon
on meadow, the hill and the shore.
They sing no more by the glimmer of the moon
on the bench by that old cabin door."

For now, though, on this cold Saturday, there was only the sound of 58,000 voices singing the hauntingly beautiful words to Stephen Foster's song. To a Kentuckian, nothing else captures so movingly the bittersweet essence of life—of loss and reminiscence, of family and the yearning for home. It is the way they say goodbye to Kentucky's seniors, but it is also the way they say hello—a message that their Kentucky home always awaits them, if only in their hearts. It is maudlin, but never corny. It runs deep in a Kentuckian's soul, intensely personal and yet communal. Decade upon decade, they've sung it before every Kentucky game, the voices rising when they come to the words:

> *"Weep no more, my lady,*
> *oh weep no more today.*
> *We will sing one song for my old Kentucky home,*
> *for my old Kentucky home far away.*

As the music ended, another emotion surged through the crowd, another lump in the throat to ponder. There was no introduction for Tim Couch. But what everyone realized—what everyone hoped against—was the distinct possibility that this would be the final home game of Couch's Kentucky career as well..

As it turned out, of course, it was his last game in Lexington—and he made it one to remember. With Kentucky tied 3-3 with Vanderbilt after one quarter, Couch threw two touchdown passes in the second quarter for a 17-3 lead, then threw three more in a 31-point Wildcat explosion in the third quarter. The final was 55-17. Couch walked off the field with statistics suitable for neon: 44 of 53 passing for 492 yards and five touchdowns.

He also walked off to pleas from the crowd. "One more year! One more year! One more year!" they chanted. As it grew in volume, Couch glanced up. In the grandstands, a sign with a new take on an old theme could be seen. "COME BACK, DEUCE," it read, "DON'T CUT US LOOSE!" A trace of a smile crossed Couch's face. But at the post-game press conference, he gave hints of what his decision would be.

"I think it's kind of neat, really, for people to care about what I'm going to do," he said. "But in a situation like this, you really have to do what's best for yourself. You kind of have to be selfish when you're making a decision like this."

Certainly there were other clues. At game's end, Elbert Couch hopped down from the stands, ran over to his son and hugged him. Still, there was no indication on Tim's face, no opening of the emotional floodgates to suggest that, yes, this was it, his last home game. As Kentucky's band played "Rhapsody in Blue," Couch jogged off the field. There would be no farewell parade. He waved his fist, and that was it. If the signals were mixed, perhaps it was because Couch's own decision was still wavering between yea and nay.

Regardless, there was the victory to savor. Kentucky was 7-3. A major bowl was now a possibility. And a major upset of Tennessee—the one game UK fans yearn to win more than any other—seemed within the realm of possibility.

Tim Couch went to sleep that night with much the same feeling. So much had been accomplished. So much more was within grasp.

The phone rang early Sunday morning. When Couch, half asleep, answered it, he struggled to make sense of the frantic, weeping voice on the other end. It was Joey

King, a UK baseball player. There'd been an accident. Scott and Artie were dead. Jason was in bad shape. How bad, he didn't know.

Later, Tim Couch would tell Terry Frei of *The Sporting News* that he tried to convince himself he was dreaming all this. "I told myself, 'Hey, this ain't real,'" he said to Frei. "I knew I was going to wake up and tell myself I hadn't really heard the horrifying news."

By 10 o'clock, however, Couch was having to relay the news to others. Dave Baker remembers:

For seven years I did a talk radio show every Sunday morning in Lexington on WVLK. The tenor of the show largely depended, of course, on what had happened during the game the previous day. When the performances were bad it was sometimes tough to field some of the more irate callers, even though it did make for good talk radio.

Sunday, November 15, 1998 was not one of those mornings—not after Kentucky had romped past Vanderbilt. There were two big issues on the table: Did Kentucky actually have a chance in the regular season finale at Tennessee; and was the Vandy game Couch's last in Commonwealth Stadium?

During a break following the first hour of the program with the second hour about to begin, my pager buzzed. On the pager's readout was a familiar number. It was Joe Gentry, Tim's uncle. I made a mental note to call him once the show was finished. I normally wouldn't get a call from Joe or Tim, who sometimes stayed overnight at his uncle's, in the middle of the show, but I had no reason for concern—until, that is, I phoned Joe Gentry.

His first words froze me.

"Dave," he said, "there's been an accident."

For a sick, fleeting moment, I was gripped by the fear that something had happened to Tim. That it hadn't been Couch was small consolation. For the next few minutes, I sat stunned as Joe relayed the awful news. Brock and Steinmetz were dead. Watts, the center with whom Couch had worked so closely and had depended on the last two seasons, was being airlifted to the UK Medical Center. His condition was unknown.

I thanked Joe for telling me, hung up, and dialed Tim's number as I'd done so many times before—not as a member of the media, but as a friend.

The voice at the other end of the line was not the voice I was used to hearing.

"I just heard the news," I told him. "How are you doing?"

"It's pretty tough right now," Tim said, his voice thick with emotion. For a private person like Couch, who uses words sparingly, his answer spoke volumes. We talked awhile longer, Tim telling me the details as he knew them—the pain as evident in the long pauses as it was in the words spoken.

There wasn't much more to say. I told him that if there was anything I could do to help, I'd be there for him. "I appreciate your calling," Tim said. It was a response as sad as it was sincere.

Couch spent the rest of that day alternating between dazed incredulity and torrents of anguish. He went to UK's medical center where Watts had been airlifted and saw him briefly. He drove to Hyden. That night, he got in bed and cried, memories of Scott Brock and the moments they'd shared dominating his consciousness. There would be little if any sleep.

Rena Vicini had gotten a call from media relations director Tony Neely at 8:30 that morning. "At that point," she says, "all we knew was that it was Jason—that he'd been driving and he was being helicoptered back to Lexington. We knew how many were involved, but we didn't know who they were."

Matt Mumme, the coach's son, had made hunting trips with Watts before. Vicini said he originally was going to go with the others that Sunday. When Hal Mumme got the news, he and his wife June were in a state of near panic.

"Hal thought it might have been Matt, because they couldn't get hold of him," Vicini says. "And I just immediately started hyperventilating and crying."

Vicini composed herself. She received another call informing her of the victims, and that Watts was on his way to the hospital. It would be her job to deal with the media there. When she arrived, she recognized some faces.

"Where's Jason?" she asked.

"Jason's in the back. They're treating him right now," someone said. "That's his father over there."

Vicini walked up to Jim Watts and introduced herself. Watts burst into tears. She held him in her arms as he sobbed and shook.

"What can I say to the parents of these two boys?" he cried out. "How can I possibly tell them how sorry I am?"

"That's what he was concerned about first—not Jason, who was badly hurt but was going to make it; but the two boys and their parents," Vicini says. "Finally, I was able to ask him about Tim. I was really concerned about him because of Scott. He said Tim had already been there."

Early that evening, athletic director C.M. Newton would hold a press conference. Mumme would not speak until the next day at his regular Monday press conference. "Hal was so distraught," Vicini says. "He couldn't deal with the media right then."

As the day wore on, player after player came to the hospital, seeking word of Watts' condition. Representatives of the media began to converge as well. The place was becoming a zoo—grief and shock mixing with the media's need to know, reporters hurling questions whenever and at whomever they could. It was all becoming too much—private grief threatening to degenerate into public circus.

"My big thing was protecting the players from the media, because they were trying to camp out at the dorms and at their apartments and trying to get into the hospital," Vicini, a former newspaper writer, says. "I basically had security get them out of the hospital. I mean, it just wasn't appropriate. All those players were coming in bawling their eyes out.

"I've been on both sides of the fence. I know what the media needs, and I'm always fighting for the media to have access—but this was totally inappropriate. So we had security keep them out of there, and we tried to keep them off the hospital property."

The week would never approach anything close to normalcy. On Monday, a time when the players would usually meet to view film before practicing, they filed into a room, sat down and said not a word. Most of them stared at the floor. Then, several of them broke into tears. Some of them, on their knees in prayer, held hands and sobbed.

The school provided psychological counseling for those who wanted it. Mumme, his face reflecting the spent emotion and lack of sleep, spoke eloquently of the fragility and preciousness of life. Soon came more troubling news. Blood testing revealed that Watts had been driving while well above the legal limit for intoxication. Later it would be known that Brock and Steinmetz were also above the limit. As if the grief and shock weren't enough, now there was this new, unsettling element to ponder.

On Tuesday they practiced again, if it can be called that. There was little studying of film, and only basic stuff run through on the field. On Wednesday they went 120 miles to Hyden for Brock's funeral, with Couch a pallbearer. They had a 9 o'clock practice that night. On Thursday morning, they filed onto three busses and headed for Covington, 90 miles away, to attend the funeral of Steinmetz. Couch, mentally exhausted and emotionally wasted after the service for his close friend, didn't make the trip. When the Steinmetz service ended, the players rode back to Lexington for another practice. On Friday, they left for Knoxville.

How do you measure grief? It followed them wherever they went. It followed them at the funerals, where people jammed into the churches and hundreds were left standing outside, watching the services on TV monitors. It followed them into classrooms, where several professors called for a moment of silence. And it followed them onto the practice field, where at least there was the chance to feign normalcy, to let the body express what the heart had held in.

It was grief piled upon grief, made worse when the news came that Watts' blood-alcohol level had tested out to 1 1/2 times the legal limit. Jail was a very real possibility. Indeed, Watts would plead guilty when his trial opened a few months later and received the maximum sentence of 10 years. Before the trial, he addressed a group of students and told his story, talked of his anguish, told them of the dangers of drinking and driving. When he pled guilty, he asked to immediately begin serving time.

Tim Couch had been close to Watts. He was his center, after all, and the heart of UK's offensive line. Watts was the one who called out blocking assignments to the rest of the line on each play. He also felt the loss of Steinmetz, an affable sort who, like Couch, loved country music. Artie had started several games as a freshman at Michigan State and had been practicing with the Kentucky team every day, awaiting the 1999 season when he'd be eligible to play again.

But worst of all was the loss of Scott Brock. Tim and Scott had been best buddies since kindergarten. In high school, Brock was a wide receiver, catching 36 of Couch's passes when they were seniors. Along with Paul Melton, Tim and Scott were captains of the team.

They were virtually inseparable. How many times had they fished together, Scott listening to Tim as he talked, for the umpteenth time, about his dream of playing in the NFL someday? Scott had come to UK along with Tim. He left after a semester to return to Hyden, then enrolled at Eastern Kentucky University, only 20 miles from Lexington. Every week during the season, Tim would make the drive to Richmond to watch "Monday Night Football" at Scott's apartment. It was easy to like Scott Brock. He'd been voted "Mr. Personality" by his classmates at Leslie County High. It hadn't taken long for many on Kentucky's team to become friends with him.

But nobody could feel the loss as heavily as Couch. You couldn't measure the grief, but you could feel it—and there was no escape.

"He was trying to put up a front," James Whalen says, "but you could see it. He was real sad and just real confused. It took a lot of desire away from him for a while. I think it did for all of us. I mean, here we were, one of our teammates is dead, and one of our good friends as well. It's just real hard to concentrate. And it makes football seem so small. It was hard to get geared up."

If there was any momentary escape, it came during the few practice sessions Kentucky held.

"I think it was really good in a way," Whalen says, "because, as an athlete, that's where we get our emotions out—on the field. It's where we can let everything else leave our minds and we're just worried about one thing. Getting back to practice so fast really helped us, as far as getting our minds right. I mean, it was still difficult, but I think that just getting out there and just trying to forget about it for two hours was something we all needed."

Still, Kentucky didn't bring the normal preparation to the week. There was little if any detail given to particulars about Tennessee. Practice provided the fleeting illusion of normalcy, but fleeting was the operative word.

"Yes, it was different," Whalen says. "There was a definite aura on the field. It wasn't a normal Tennessee game week."

It was on Monday of that week, two days before he would help put Scott Brock in the ground, when Tim Couch talked to the media. He'd driven to Hyden to console the Brocks and be consoled by his own family, then drove back for the team meeting and practice.

"We asked the players if anyone wanted to talk," Vicini says. "We weren't going to make anybody talk. Everybody was going to be off limits if that's how they wanted it.

But Tony (Neely) went into the locker room and asked if anybody wanted to volunteer. Five players agreed to do it."

One of them was Couch.

"You could tell that the reason he did was because he wanted to talk about Scott," Vicini says.

He spoke about all the things the two had done together. He spoke haltingly, heavily. Finally, Vicini broke in. "One more question," she said.

"And Chuck Culpepper asked him something. I can't even remember the question," Vicini says. "And I don't think Tim really was answering the question. He just started talking about how every time now when he's riding in his car and he hears a song, it reminds him of Scott. And then he just started bawling. I said, 'That's it,' and I hugged him. Somebody gave him a handkerchief, and everybody just backed away."

Vicini, who always attended Kentucky's away games and made it a point to never miss the Tennessee game in particular, did not go to Knoxville. She stayed at the hospital, keeping company with Watts and distributing news to the media as it warranted. But there was another reason she didn't go.

"I knew we had no shot," she says. "I didn't even want to watch it on TV."

Dave Baker recalls what it was like for Tim Couch in Neyland Stadium before the crowd of more than 100,000 people filed in:

After they arrived at the stadium, the players went onto the field in street clothes—taking their customary walk around the place before suiting up. There was Couch, tossing a ball back and forth with some teammates as he made his way over seemingly every blade of grass.

If it hadn't been obvious before, it was crystal clear now. Couch knew he had to do all the other things associated with football—going to class, meeting the media, acting and carrying himself in certain way. But this was what he loved— being in the arena, being part of the game.

At least he had this moment where he could lose him-self—back on a football field, back in the battle. But things were different. The week had been a blur of grief and confusion and questions with no answers. Now there was a game to be played, against Kentucky's biggest rival, against the nation's top-ranked and unbeaten team. It was the sort of challenge he loved the most. But this just wasn't the same.

His heart told him to hope for the best.

His head told him to expect the worst.

It is June 1999, seven months later, and Hal Mumme is being asked what role the tragedy played in the Kentucky-Tennessee game. "It obviously affected the game," the questioner says, "but in retrospect—"

Mumme doesn't wait for the questioner to finish.

"I don't remember *any* of it," he says. "You know, if you've ever been in a car wreck or a tragedy or something where you really get shook up … you know how you kind of get in this mild form of shock—where when you look back on it, after a good period of time, there's just a lot of things about it you don't remember? That's the way that week was for me.

"And Tim was just like the rest of us. We were all in shock. I think most of our guys played that whole game in shock."

Whalen agrees. "I think I remember maybe one play from that game, and that's it. It was so hard to focus and keep concentration. I would love to play Tennessee again in a normal week. We weren't ready to play. I mean, normally we're in there watching hours and hours worth of film, getting ready, planning, practicing, all that stuff. We went to two funerals that week. We didn't watch hardly any film. I mean, I didn't know what Tennessee was going to do."

"We were either going to win or get the crap beat out of us," Tom Kalinowski, the equipment manager, says. "Everybody was in a little bit of a state that week, Tim more than the others. You could see it in his eyes. You never know how kids are going to react to something like that. Sometimes it's a rallying point and sometimes kids just kind of fall apart.

"Of course, the fact we were playing the eventual national champion had something to do with it. When it all comes down to it, Tennessee was pretty damned good."

Both factors were at work, of course. Although Kentucky actually jumped to a 7-6 lead on a 3-yard pass from Couch to Lance Mickelsen, the Vols were in the midst of a stampede. After punting on their first series, Tennessee scored the next eight times it got the ball. It was 38-7 at halftime, 52-14 at the end of three quarters, and 59-21 at game's end.

Without Watts to call the blocking assignments, Tennessee took advantage of huge gaps and often blitzed— mostly between the guards and center, and mostly untouched. Aaron Daniel, trying to fill Watts' considerable shoes, had his problems early. Although pass protection improved later in the game, Couch was either sacked or hurried into passes that failed when things were falling completely apart in the first half. Still, he finished with 337 yards passing, completing 35 of 56 for two touchdowns with one interception.

Looking back now, Couch says that the death of his friend changed him, made him realize what's important and what isn't. Football would remain his passion. But life would never be the same. Life would be more precious, with the knowledge that nothing is promised beyond the breath you'd just taken—the breath that might be your last. With something so fragile, it seemed foolhardy not to respect the gift. All those timeless questions of life and death, of finding meaning, were no longer just concepts to set aside for another day, for an older man to ponder. In their minds, young men are bulletproof. In the loss he endured, Tim Couch learned otherwise.

"I think we all found out a lot of things about each other and about ourselves that week," Mumme says. "It was one of those times where faith takes over and you find out what you're really made of. What you truly believe deep down inside comes out. I found out a lot about Tim. I found out a lot about many of them.

"Tim and I talked about prayer and God's plan for your life. Everybody second guesses things in times like that. Everybody questions."

A shining moment endures. In the midst of the sorrow and, yes, the controversy once it was learned that Watts had been driving while intoxicated, the parents of

Artie Steinmetz did a remarkable thing. At the funeral of their son, they invited Jason Watts' parents to sit with them at the front of the church. Visibly moved, Mumme made a point to tell the media about it later that week. He wanted to shed light on the nobility of the act—and the selflessness Marshall and Therese Steinmetz had displayed in the forgiveness they'd offered, all this in an era when lawsuits strangle the landscape like so many weeds.

"That was one of the most glowing examples of caring and empathy I have ever seen," Mumme says. "It was good Christian faith."

When Watts was sentenced on April 21, 1999, to 10 years in jail, it was the Steinmetz family, Mumme says, who continued to help in the legal process. Jailed on March 31 after he had pled guilty, Watts was granted shock probation and released on July 19. Judge Daniel Venters cited Watts' early acceptance of responsibility for the deaths as a key factor.

"I just hope," James Whalen says, "that everyone learned from it and grows a little bit because of it."

And the lesson learned?

"That life isn't fair," Whalen says. "My mom has told me that since I was two years old. It was really weird, going to watch your friend being buried. You're just like, 'Wow. You're not going to live forever. You're not immortal. Anything can happen.' You know, I could walk out this door right now and get hit in the head and die. It makes you live your life every day to the fullest and thank God for what you've been given—and live your life accordingly."

For months afterward, Couch would have momentary lapses, thinking Scott Brock was still alive, expecting the friend who'd always been there to still be there. Reality would shake him awake—leaving him with the same thoughts and the same lessons that James Whalen had learned.

There was still a bowl game to play. There was still a decision to make, to stay for his senior season at Kentucky or leave for the NFL. Through it all, Couch would be looking through older eyes. They were the eyes of someone who understood what true loss was. They were the eyes of someone whose world was no longer just football.

9

1-1-99: Mission Accomplished

New Year's Day is Nirvana for college football fans—touchdowns, turnovers and tension (and the not-so-occasional hangover) running from morning to well past midnight. To the Kentucky football fan, though, this annual smorgasbord has had little significance except to show the vast chasm that still separated UK from the nation's best teams.

It had been four decades, a total of 47 years in all, since Kentucky had played in a New Year's Day Bowl. Even though they were only in the second year of a dramatically different system run by a risk-taking coach, January 1 had been the stated goal of UK's players for months.

When the team worked out in the winter of 1998, when the only thing to hit was the weight room and the books, they wore gray tee shirts with "1-1-99" across the front. If it had seemed pretentious back then, it had blossomed into serious possibility by the time Kentucky had clobbered Vanderbilt to raise its record to 7-3.

The horror of the accident and the blowout loss to Tennessee had seemingly crushed those dreams—rendering them, at least in the short run, meaningless. In the immediate aftermath of that lost week, the question of New Year's Day wasn't much discussed. But in Tampa, Florida, where officials of the Outback Bowl were deciding their choice of opponents, there were sound reasons to put Kentucky high on the list.

The Outback matches a Big Ten team against a representative from the SEC. With traditional powers such as Auburn and Alabama struggling, Kentucky moved up the ladder. Georgia, of course, was a serious possibility, and while Georgia had beaten Kentucky, the game had gone down to the final play. Furthermore, the Bulldogs, who played in the Outback the previous year, had not brought a particularly large number of fans with them. Indeed, no Outback Bowl had ever been a sellout.

Kentucky not only had a reputation for having a huge crowd following in bowl games—more than 35,000 had followed the team to Atlanta for the 1976 Peach Bowl—it also had Couch, who might be playing in his final college game.

It also probably didn't hurt that Outback Steakhouse, the bowl's primary sponsor, had as its owner and CEO none other than Chris Sullivan, a University of Kentucky graduate. Sullivan maintained throughout the process that he was just another member of the selection committee, with no more votes than any other member. But his influence obviously could have played a factor—particularly given the other compelling reasons to choose UK.

And so it came to pass that the Outback would match Kentucky against Penn State, on 11 a.m. in Raymond James

Stadium—the impressive new facility of the Tampa Bay Buccaneers—on New Year's Day. The goal of 1-1-99 had been realized. With several weeks to put some distance between themselves and the tragedy, Kentucky's players had time to re-focus on football and savor the satisfaction of a mission accomplished.

As it turned out, the game proved a beaut—not only in terms of being a competitive contest, but also as a numbers game. Kentucky sent a crowd estimated at more than 40,000 to Tampa, giving the Outback its first-ever sellout with an attendance of 66,005.

There were a number of different dynamics leading up to the game.

Penn State viewed the bowl as a bit of a letdown, given the Nittany Lions' annual goal of winning the Big Ten and competing for a national championship. Joe Paterno knew it would be difficult to get his young but talented squad ready, particularly after some of the players had spoken publicly that they were less than enthusiastic about heading to the Outback.

Nothing is more certain, however, than a Joe Paterno-coached team being ready for a bowl game. The King of the postseason, Paterno would be coaching in his 29th bowl game in 33 years as the head man in Happy Valley—a mark that tied him with Bear Bryant for first on the all-time list. During those first 28 appearances, Paterno's teams had compiled a sparkling 18-9-1 record.

For Hal Mumme, of course, the situation was just the opposite. Mumme had lots of experience in the playoffs at the high school, NAIA and NCAA Division II levels. But this was his first jump into the deep water of a big-time bowl.

It was great exposure for the young coach and his young program at a key recruiting time of the year. More than that, it gave him an abundance of extra practice time—which he used in part to take long looks at backup quarterbacks should Couch depart, a prospect Mumme believed to be just shy of a foregone conclusion, though he wasn't saying it publicly.

It wasn't until Kentucky arrived in the Tampa area some two weeks before the game that he focused on Penn State. There was the usual fun and games for the players as well—including "team day" at Busch Gardens amusement park.

Those who were there saw the unthinkable. They saw Tim Couch flinch.

"The folks at the park wanted to take some photos of Tim," UK quarterback coach Chris Hatcher says. "Tim said that was fine—*until* they said that they wanted to get the shots while he was riding in the roller coaster and up in the front car.

"That's when he tried to outsmart 'em and said, 'I'd rather not without my teammates.' Heck, he just didn't want to ride on that coaster."

Maybe so, which only lent irony to the fact that, when game day came, Tim Couch would go eye to eye and helmet to helmet with some fearsome Penn State defensive players—All America linebacker Lavar Arrington, in particular—and launch himself into collisions without a second thought.

It was a grand stage from which Couch would ultimately be making his exit from the collegiate game. It was also Kentucky's first New Year's Day game since the 1952 Cotton Bowl, when Babe Parilli, the most famous Kentucky quarterback prior to Couch, threw for two touchdowns in a 20-7 win over Texas Christian. UK's coach at the time was Bear Bryant.

Mumme is as opposite a number to Bryant as Buffett is to Beethoven, of course. There is little hitting in practice, no full-scale scrimmages in the pre-season August workouts and more a sense of collaboration than commandeering in his relationship with players. It had served him particularly well with Couch, their communication producing tactics in the heat of battle that had consistently brought results.

January 1, 1999 was a glorious morning in Tampa. Beautiful sunshine, a cloudless sky and temperatures in the low 70s with a slight breeze coming in from the bay. With the gates still closed to the public, Dave Baker stood on the field. He recalls what happened next:

It's customary for Mumme's teams to get onto the field about 90 minutes before kickoff. I always like to be down there to get a feel for things. But on this day, at about 9:15 in the morning, still before Kentucky usually shows up, I turned to hear footsteps and there was Tim Couch, leading the team onto the field.

Couch is like most of us: the later we can sleep in, the more we like it. His passion for mornings off during his junior year was obvious in his class schedule, which mixed late afternoon sessions with early evening classes after practice.

"When's the last time you were up this early?" I asked Couch.

"The last time I was squirrel huntin'," he said.

Having seen him so many times in so many pre-game situations like this, it was apparent that Couch was more than ready.

So was the amazing contingent of Kentucky fans, which began to stream in, completely filling their designated side of the stadium and most of the other side. When he opened the ESPN telecast of the game, play-by-play announcer Ron Franklin said, "I went to bed in the state of Florida last night and woke up in the state of Kentucky."

Most of the experts—including the coaches themselves—had broken the game down to a battle of tempo. Could Kentucky get the Air Raid going and keep those big Penn State linebackers off balance by mixing it with draws to Derek Homer and short dump-offs to Anthony White? And could a patchwork offensive line give Couch enough time?

A unit that began the season with five seniors had been reduced to only three, with two redshirt freshmen, Matt Brown and Nolan DeVaughn, now starting. DeVaughn replaced Daniel, who'd been ineffective replacing Watts in the Tennessee game, and Brown had replaced Jonas Liening, dismissed from the team earlier in the season. At least Brown had the benefit of having started Kentucky's last three games—but against Penn State, Kentucky's line was suddenly both thin and green.

If Kentucky hoped to keep Penn State off balance, the Nittany Lions aimed to inflict their own brand of vertigo on Couch by knocking him off his feet. The other part of the equation was to keep those feet mostly on the sidelines with a physical, Big Ten grind-em-out offense that would eat up the clock.

Kentucky had excellent front line talent—particularly on offense—but the lack of depth and a defense that still looked susceptible at times raised questions. Penn State also had the edge in bowl experience, of course. Not that

Kentucky's players appeared wide-eyed and just pleased to be in such a game. To the contrary, after Penn State won the toss and deferred, when the official asked Couch if his team wanted the ball, his response was an animated, "Oh, yeah!"

Not surprisingly, Couch's first pass was a completion—a seven-yard gain to James Whalen. But the offense couldn't get a first down and had to punt, and that's when the first test came. Jimmy Carter's kick was blocked. Penn State took over at the UK 37. But when Travis Forney missed a 51-yard field goal, the Wildcats had dodged the proverbial bullet.

Throughout the year, Kentucky had been a dominant offensive team, especially in the first quarter—so it was crucial that they make something happen early. It came on the next possession when Hal Mumme once again went for it on fourth down (In all, Mumme went for it 77 times in his first two years, against the 80 times he elected to punt.) This time it was vintage stuff. On fourth-and-two from the Penn State 48, Couch faked a handoff on a reverse to Quentin McCord sprinting to the left, then handed off for real to Yeast on a reverse to the right. Yeast, who would only catch two passes for 31 yards all day, gained six yards to keep the drive alive.

What soon followed was the kind of play that has made Couch a legend in Kentucky—and should have made critics of his arm strength question their powers of reason. Rolling out of the pocket from a heavy rush and running to his left, Couch threw across his body, unable to fully plant on his back foot for leverage. Not that it mattered. It was a long-range bullet. Near the back of the end zone, it carried just over Penn State's defenders and into the arms of a leaping Lance Mickelsen. The touchdown went into the books as a 37-yard pass. But the throw itself had carried just a yard or so shy of 50—accomplished virtually all through sheer arm strength. Kentucky led, 7-0.

After Penn State's Tony Stewart dropped a sure touchdown pass and the Lions settled for a field goal to cut the lead to 7-3, Couch continued in a deadly rhythm. He led Kentucky on a 64-yard scoring drive capped by a short out pass to White, who made one of his typical now-you-have-me, now-you-don't moves to sidestep a defender and coast into the end zone. The play covered 16 yards.

Penn State had given up only two first-quarter touchdowns its entire season. But there the Lions stood, yielding two to Kentucky and Couch and trailing 14-3 with 1:47 to go in the first period. Couch had hit 10 of 11 passes. So much for this being a mismatch. In the radio booth, Dave Baker saw something that underscored the seriousness of the Penn State situation:

Just to the right of the UK booth was the Penn State announcing team that included Joe Paterno's brother, George. He was really starting to get a little hot around the collar. And the better Kentucky got, the more George kept getting something to drink from his briefcase. One might assume it wasn't a Pepsi.

"You don't get any better than they were the first couple of drives they had the football," Joe Paterno would say after the game. "They kept their poise and we panicked. They kept discipline on defense. So I was pleased with the way we came through that. That's the first time we've been in a real tough football game where we really hung in there, so that was a good sign."

It was good for the Lions, bad for the Cats. In particular, Penn State—which had tried to pressure Couch with blitzes only to be torn to shreds—began mixing it up, often rushing only three and dropping eight into coverage.

Early in the second quarter, Courtney Brown sacked Couch as he tried to throw out of his end zone. An offsides penalty nullified the safety, but from that point on the Penn State defense was able to make a play when it needed it most. Paterno's club still got the ball in great field position and required only two plays to go 56 yards and pull within four at 14-10.

Once again, a big play set up Kentucky. Yeast came right back with an Outback Bowl-record 67-yard kickoff return. But Couch, arching a ball nicely to find Dougie Allen on an out pattern, had it intercepted when Anthony King cut in front, jumped and made a brilliant tightrope walk near the sideline as he came down with the ball in his hands.

What followed, however, was one of the most extraordinary displays of talent and grit that Couch had ever summoned. That it came within a whisker of giving Kentucky a 21-10 lead at a time when Penn State's defense had all the momentum—a display which may well have changed the course of the game—made it all the more thrilling. And, ultimately, all the more frustrating for Kentucky fans pondering "What if?"

It started on third-and-26 from the UK 4. Dropping into the end zone to pass, Couch shot up the middle to escape a heavy rush, somehow darted between a Penn State defensive back and linemen who was closing in from the side at full speed at the 20, and then dropped his shoulder to knock a defensive back onto the ground at the 34. The 30-yard run was Couch's longest of the season. Later in the same drive, on third-and-one, he scrambled up the middle for nine to the Penn State 35.

Soon came the fateful play.

Kentucky faced fourth-and-14 from the 39 and went for it. Couch lofted a perfect pass to a streaking Yeast, the closest man to him another UK receiver. But it was close to high noon, and in looking into the bright sky, Yeast was blinded. Trying to intuit when the ball would reach him, he brought his hands in an instant too soon, catching only air as the ball sailed just beyond him. Once upon a time, Hal Mumme and Tim Couch had looked into the sky and the stars had whispered victory. This time, Craig Yeast had looked into the sky and the sun had pulled a fast one.

The game would remain tight well into the fourth quarter—but if ever there were a turning point, it was this. (Kentucky fans would also look back grimly at a pass interference call against Penn State inside the Lions' 10-yard line that was reversed by the officials, ruining another UK threat.)

Kentucky did get another golden chance after Ronnie Riley recovered a bobble by Eric McCoo in Penn State territory. But Couch, scrambling again and looking uncertain whether to run or throw, ended up floating his pass well over the head of Allen, and again King picked it off.

Couch's great scramble out of his end zone had ended with some spirited chest bumping and high fives with his teammates. Later, when he would again scramble and meet three Penn State players, including the formidable Arrington, head-on—blasting into them to get a first down—Couch sprang to his feet and signalled first down.

"I just seen an opening and kind of took off," Couch said afterwards. "And I knew those guys were gonna get physical once I got out there, so I was trying to bring the contact to them before they could hit me. I love playing the game and I just react out of pure love for the game. I wasn't trying to be derogatory toward them. It was just kind of havin' a good time. I like playing football, and that's the way it is."

You *had* to love the game to take the kind of pounding that Couch endured. He was sacked six times and went to the ground in some form or fashion virtually every time he threw the ball.

Once in particular, he was crushed by a blitzing Arrington. Months later, sitting in for an Internet Q&A with fans, he said the hit by Arrington was the hardest one he'd ever taken. He was pretty much of that mind minutes after the game.

"He got me pretty good," Couch said at the time. "He knocked the breath out of me for a little bit. But he's a great player. I talked to him a few times in between plays, and he also seemed like a great person when he wasn't trying to tear my head off."

Indeed, after one big hit, you could see Couch saying something to Arrington after they'd both gotten up, both of them smiling at the exchange, Couch giving him a congratulatory tap on the top of his helmet. Warriors respect warriors.

Kentucky was clinging to a 14-13 lead when the first half ended, but Forney hit a field goal to put Penn State ahead for good in the third quarter. Arrington blocked a 30-yard field goal attempt by Kentucky's Hanson, and Penn State added another field goal to lead 19-14 heading into the final 15 minutes

The Nittany Lions and defensive coordinator Jerry Sandusky had done what no other team had done all season—shutting down the Air Raid after one quarter. On the other hand, UK defensive coordinator Mike Major and his unit had played better than most expected—particularly in red zone situations—to keep the Wildcats in the game. But they appeared to be tiring now.

That's why, early in the fourth quarter with his team only down by five, Mumme again went for it on fourth-and-one at the UK 35. That, and the fact that Kentucky's punting game had been horrible. Homer was stopped short on a run up the middle, however, and Penn State, converting on a fourth-and-one of its own at the UK 26, got a touchdown to lead 26-14.

"I don't question going for it," Mumme said. "But I do question the call. I made a really bad call. We did it the next time we were down there and made it fairly easy, so it was a poor call on my part."

Mumme had developed a reputation as a riverboat gambler—and he certainly has many of the attributes. Was it foolhardy under the circumstances? Some thought so, although there's at least the notion that he simply had a good idea of what the other guy had in his hand. More to the point, he knew how much—or rather, how little—he was holding himself at the time.

"You could tell in the third quarter that their size and strength and maturity was just taking its toll on us," he said. "You got to know how many bullets you've got left to fire on defense, and that's what I try to keep track of."

Kentucky would mount one more drive when there was a chance of drawing within five with still enough time on the clock to get the ball back and win, but it ended on downs in Penn State territory. Couch would finish 30-of-48 passing for 336 yards, two touchdowns and two interceptions.

His last collegiate pass came on the last play of the game, a completion to Jimmy Robinson. But Penn State stripped Robinson of the ball and Anthony King nearly returned it for a touchdown.

There were two UK players rushing over near the goal line to stop King.

One of them was lineman Mike Webster, who made the hit on the run to knock King down.

The other one—the guy right by Webster's side and matching him stride for stride—was Tim Couch.

For someone who would soon weigh the decision to turn pro and decide it was time, this seemed a fitting end, the perfect definition of Tim Couch's career. He'd completed the last pass he would ever attempt in college, and here he was, going above and beyond the call again, rushing over to attempt a tackle on a play that didn't matter. Didn't matter, of course, except for Kentucky's players and its fans. Didn't matter, except that it embodied the very passion for the game that Couch exudes.

"I thought he was brilliant all year and we wouldn't have been in a New Years Day bowl if wasn't for Tim,"

Mumme said moments after the game. "He's been a lot of fun to coach. And I hope to coach him for another year."

His head told him otherwise, of course. Later, at the press conference Couch held to announce he was leaving, Mumme would say that he knew Couch would leave before even Couch knew it, that he sensed it before the season began. Couch, meanwhile, would thank Mumme, noting that if it hadn't been for the coach, he probably would never have stayed at Kentucky.

Despite the defeat, it had been a season to remember. 1-1-99 was a reality. Kentucky had finished 7-5, but had been closer to doing much, much more. And in the respectability of the battle they'd waged against Penn State, they'd been able to free themselves up for football again, to move out from under the emotional weight of the tragedy that had visited them only a few weeks before.

"The goal that we seniors had was to get the program back on track," said Rhodes scholar nominee and leading tackler Jeff Zurcher. "We would have set a great standard if we would have won, instead of a good standard by getting here."

Mumme himself, who wasn't that far removed from the days when he was both coaching teams and washing their uniforms as well, had just been given a new five-year contract. The deal, which would run through December 31, 2003, was reportedly worth $4 million, replacing Mumme's old deal of $450,000 per season.

"The signing of this contract serves notice that we are staying at UK," Mumme said, referring not only to himself but to his wife, June. "I hope this puts an end to any speculation about me being interested in any other positions at the present time, and in the future."

But would Tim Couch serve notice that he was staying, too? It was the main question reporters asked.

"When I get home," Couch replied, "I'll have a few days to make a good decision and just see where I'm at."

But the die had already been cast. One week later, the announcement became official. He was leaving for the pros.

The key factor was hardly a surprise. Couch read the tea leaves, checked which way the wind was blowing and ascertained that, yes, his chances of going No. 1 in the NFL draft were good. In fact, they appeared to be very, very good.

How could he have said no to that? It was the dream he'd held as a child, the goal he'd written into his notebook as a boy. And now, the young man of 21 had the goal in sight—had it, in fact, right in the crosshairs.

Little did he know then that, in the high pressure stakes and endless histrionics that surround the NFL draft, the goal would remain in doubt until the very morning the draft was held.

10

The $59 Million Question

Elbert Couch needed some time to himself. Back home he might have gone down by the creek or retreated to the garage where the skillets and saws lined the walls. But this was New York City. He walked out of his hotel and headed toward Times Square, the man from Thousandsticks lost in the panoply of a thousand skyscrapers. Which is how he wanted it. Elbert Couch sought anonymity. On the sidewalks of New York he found it. For almost four hours he walked them—worry his only companion.

"If he doesn't go number one," Elbert told himself, "he's made a mistake."

It was the day before the NFL draft would be held in Madison Square Garden. Negotiations between the Cleveland Browns and Tim's agent, Tom Condon, were still going on. Tim had made it no secret that he wanted to play for the Browns. It was more than that, of course. Elbert remembered when his youngest son, still in grade school, had come up to him and said that his goal was to be the No. 1 draft pick in the NFL someday.

Now it was about to happen. Or was it? Less than 24 hours to go, and that was the question—a $59 million question, as it turned out. But for now, there was still no decision from the Browns, still no end to the haggling and the bluffing and the passions that sometimes bubbled to the boiling point.

"I found out later," Elbert says, "that it got pretty testy between Tom (Condon) and the Cleveland negotiators. I think it got to be a screaming match or something. You can't be a good guy all the time."

You can't be a calm and collected guy all the time, either—not when doubt still surrounded the outcome of Tim Couch's dream. "You always want your sons to be number one, no matter what," Elbert says. "Tim had always wanted this. If he hadn't been projected as being number one, I don't think he would have come out early."

By now, he figured, the Browns would have decided. The deal should have been done. It appeared to be coming down to Couch and Akili Smith, the strong-armed quarterback from Oregon. But still the talks dragged on. In the hotel, people kept walking up to Elbert Couch, asking him for news.

"I didn't want that," he says. "That's the reason I got out in Times Square, where nobody knew me. I started at about one o'clock that afternoon and just walked around until about five. I kept thinking negative things. All the negatives—that if he didn't go number one, he'd made a mistake. He might have wanted to go back to Kentucky."

This was worse, Elbert figured, than that night when he'd waited until the wee hours to hear his son's choice of schools. So he walked, another face in a sea of faces, fearing the worst—trying to get lost in his thoughts without getting lost in the bad part of town, without even knowing, of course, which part was the bad part.

Cleveland held other appeal. In Browns fans still wounded from Art Modell moving the team to Baltimore and renaming them the Ravens (the average Browns fan would tell you that Vultures would have been more appropriate) Couch could enjoy the same passionate and loyal base in Cleveland that he'd experienced at Kentucky. Brought back into the NFL as an expansion team, they'd be starting from scratch, trying to regain the glory of decades long gone. It was a familiar format for Couch, who had helped turn around a Kentucky program which hadn't seen glory days since the 1950s.

Couch had seen Rick Pitino become almost deified in the Commonwealth when he came to Lexington after an NCAA probation had crippled Kentucky basketball; he later brought it a sixth national championship. While not to the same degree, Couch had much the same effect on Wildcat football.

Before his breakout year of 1997, about the only place in Lexington where you could find a Kentucky football uniform was in Tom Kalinowski's equipment room. But once Couch emerged and Hal Mumme's offense got on a rollicking roll, there were tee shirts, hats, car flags and jerseys—especially the ones with 2 on them—not only in sporting goods stores, but in every mom and pop gas station from border to border.

Couch knew, then, what it was like to have everyone's hopes riding on his shoulders. Rather than feeling its weight, he relished its challenge. In Cleveland, he could see himself facing the same music. Drew Carey, after all, can only do so much. Cleveland rocks. Couch would help it roll.

"Tim went to Kentucky when it obviously wasn't on top of the world in football," Elbert Couch says. "And he told me, 'Daddy, I believe I can go down there and help.' He didn't say he could go down there and change the program on his own. He said he believed he could help change it. Then he got some good players around him—Craig Yeast, some of those guys—and they did change it. Now he wanted to help with a new franchise going back into the NFL. He wanted to start out new and help build something."

Behind the good old boy exterior, genuine as it may be, there was more than just sentiment at work. Couch had done his homework. For one thing, he knew that of all the teams that might pick him, Cleveland would give him the best chance of making his lofty dreams come true.

Philadelphia, picking second, didn't have a chance to be as good as fast as the Browns might become, thanks to liberal expansion rules—the same set of guidelines that earlier in the decade propelled both Carolina and Jacksonville into the playoffs early in their existence.

Cincinnati, picking third, already had a bunch of quarterbacks under contract—and rightly or wrongly, general manager Mike Brown had developed a reputation as being a nightmare for first round picks to deal with. That tag would not abandon him after Akili Smith, who wound up with the Bengals, missed most of pre-season camp when negotiations stalled.

Couch was also smart enough never to talk about any of this publicly. No bad mouthing other teams, no posturing that he *deserved* the number one pick. All he said was that he wanted to play for the Browns, and in that he was sincere. In 1999, there was no question the Browns were the perfect fit.

Browns fans had spent three years in limbo. It had felt like three lifetimes. Many of them had followed the team for years, enduring the brutal cold of the winds off Lake Erie in November, sitting in a vast but aging stadium where sideline seats were far removed from the playing field—and loving every minute of it.

Understanding the Browns' heritage and the city's passion for the team, Couch saw an opportunity to carve a unique place for himself in the franchise's proud history. If the Browns were being reborn, what better situation than to figure prominently in their growth into a force again?

It would not be the first time a Kentuckian had figured in Cleveland's football success. Blanton Collier had been Paul Brown's right hand man during the glory days. In the 1950s he took a cut in pay to become Kentucky's head coach—because that was his boyhood dream. But he later returned to the Browns and became head coach, leading them to NFL championships.

Now another was seeking to come to Cleveland after choosing to be at Kentucky out of sentiment and boyhood dreams. Now there was a striking new stadium being built by the lake, with a new owner, Al Lerner, who seemed willing to pay whatever it took to fill his organization with the best football people he could find.

In many respects, Cleveland Browns football is like college football—with loyal fans and loyal ex-players. Probably nowhere else in the league (Green Bay included) is there a more tightly knit group of "alumni" who stay as active with the club and the community. The Browns offices are located on Lou Groza Boulevard. On the night of the team's re-entry into the NFL in the Hall of Fame exhibition game in Canton, more than 20 former players were on hand to join in the celebration.

The list of Browns greats reads like a football *Who's Who*. There's the incomparable Jim Brown. There's Leroy Kelly. But the televangelist of this revival would always be the quarterback. From Otto Graham to Brian Sipe and most assuredly to Bernie Kosar, Cleveland fans adore their quarterbacks. Kosar, in particular, epitomizes what those fans who inhabit the Dawg Pound are all about. A native of northern Ohio, Kosar is hard working, demanding and fiercely loyal. Kosar currently serves as a Browns advisor, but his most important role may be as the club's unofficial ambassador. Whenever he makes an appearance or his name is called over the PA system, Cleveland crowds roar. He is the link to the Browns' glittering past.

Couch, of course, is its shining hope for the future. It was a fit that football observers saw long before the official announcement that he was leaving Kentucky was ever made.

"Carmen Policy and Dwight Clark know you don't force feed quarterbacks," said ESPN draft analyst Mel Kiper Jr. on the day of the Heisman Trophy ceremony at New York's Downtown Athletic Club—which Couch attended as a finalist. Virtually everyone at the ceremony knew that Ricky Williams would leave with the statue, but, like Kiper, most were equally confident that Couch would be number one in the draft if he decided to pass up his senior season.

"They'll be an expansion team, so the expectation level won't be high," Kiper said. "There won't be pressure on Tim Couch to be the guy to turn things around because you're starting from the bottom, you're building. So for Couch, it's a great situation. The fans in Cleveland are the best. Great fans—unbelievable energy that they generate, and a new stadium going up. It seems like a perfect fit."

As soon as he declared publicly that he would not return for his senior season at Kentucky, Couch began what can only be called an all-out campaign to be the Browns' first choice. His first trip to Cleveland, in fact, came on the same day that he held his press conference at UK to announce his decision. This trip wasn't to meet with the Browns, but rather to decide on whether to have the powerful International Management Group represent him.

"We got up to Cincinnati and got snowed in," says Greg Couch. "We waited for hours in the airport, and finally the flight was canceled."

That didn't deter IMG, which dispatched a private jet to Cincinnati to fetch their man. "But we still had to circle around a couple of hours because the weather was so bad," Greg says. "When we finally got in, though, we had a great time."

To say the least. Leading point for IMG in this effort was Condon, a former NFL player turned agent. In the world of "big time" sports agents, Condon was a comer. Leigh Steinberg may have gotten more publicity, to the point of being involved in the movie *Jerry Maguire*, but in 1998 it was Condon who landed for IMG the biggest NFL prize—Peyton Manning, the Tennessee quarterback who'd gone first in the draft.

Now he was trying to do the same with Couch. Condon would negotiate the contract and Peter Johnson of IMG would handle all of the marketing efforts on Couch's behalf. Not only do they know how to put deals together, they know how to close them as well—which is why they were so interested in getting Tim and Greg into Cleveland that night despite the horrible conditions. After all, it's not every day you get to have dinner with Joe Montana.

"I probably sat there with my jaw dropped open for the first ten minutes," Greg Couch says. "Then I started realizing that he was just an ordinary guy who just happened to be the best at what he did. But it was hard to get over that. I mean, we were getting to meet one of our heroes when we were growing up. He sat there and told us stories and after we started laughing, we got kind of comfortable with him. It was great just to sit there and hear him talk about some of the things you'd seen him do on TV as a kid."

What wasn't so great was the fallout from others who'd been seeking a piece of Couch's financial pie. Not too long before the draft, a scathing article about Couch's selection of an agent appeared in the April 5, 1999 edition of *ESPN The Magazine*. Written by Tom Friend and titled "Reel to Real," it focused on the complaints of a West Coast-based agent named Gary Wichard, who basically accused Couch of going back on a commitment to make him in charge of Couch's off-the-field ventures.

Wichard seemed to regard himself as some sort of benevolent Milton Drysdale, put on the planet to rescue Jed Clampett and the rest of the Beverly Hillbillies from the financial sharks. At one point the article says that "Wichard met with Couch's brother Greg and concluded, 'We're all on the same page.' He planned a visit to Couch's parents in Hyden 'to prove I could go there and step in cow shit.' "

Apparently unaware that tripping the light fantastic in bovine excrement is not exactly high on the list of things to do in Hyden, Wichard and his claims only served to awaken the Couches to the reality of how ugly things can get when people are fighting over millions of dollars.

Greg Couch, who serves as Tim's advisor and as a liason between Tim and IMG, called the article "pretty far off the mark."

"I know that Wichard and Tom Friend, the guy who wrote the article, were pretty close friends," Greg says. "He told us that all along, that he was going to get Tim on the cover of the magazine because his buddy works for them. So there's a lot of things that go into things. Unfortunately, people believe most of what they read."

Why did Wichard lose out? Simple. Because, Greg says, they found a better situation with IMG.

"He called me from the start," Greg says. "He called me every day, sometimes twice a day. I liked Gary and I thought he would have done a good job with the contract, but looking at the overall thing, he just didn't have what IMG had with the marketing and all the rest. When he started getting into his marketing side of it and what his ideas were on the financial stuff, I didn't feel nearly as comfortable with him as I did with the other guys.

"That article really got to me because Wichard said a lot of things that were just a big—[he stops himself] but there was nothin' much you could do about it."

Rather than concentrating on damage control or stewing over the public relations hit they were taking, the brothers simply did what they had been doing all of their young lives: getting on with the next task facing them.

With IMG in control of negotiations and fielding the growing stream of calls for endorsements and commercial offers, Tim and Greg Couch focused on getting Tim ready to impress the Browns in a private workout. There were a few days down in Orlando when Tim worked with other IMG clients in what amounted to a pre-draft workout seminar, but in the mountains of Eastern Kentucky and on the blue-grass of Lexington, it was Greg who Tim prepared with, Greg who Tim confided in.

"That probably helped him more than anything," Elbert Couch says.

To take on the job as an advisor and liason for his brother, however, Greg Couch would be giving up a career he'd just begun in football. He was an assistant coach at Madison Central High in Richmond, and he and his wife were just getting ready to start a family. Could he have imagined making such a dramatic change, to drop every-thing and work for his brother?

"I guess I probably thought about it," Greg says. "I guess when somebody gets in the situation where they need somebody they can openly trust above everybody else ... Tim's got good people around him and everything, but you still need that one person that you've known and you know that, no matter what happens, if it's important, you can trust them above all else."

First on their list was getting Tim ready for his work-out with the Browns. As is customary with the picks at the top of the draft list, Couch would not work out at the league combine in Indianapolis, only taking a physical. Back in Lexington, the brothers weren't just lifting and running and throwing. They were actually scripting an entire workout designed to show off Tim's proficiency in every area of the passing game. They also got some UK receivers to participate in the workout.

By most accounts from the Couch camp, the workout—which was done in private—went well. Local newspapers also portrayed it that way. But a short time later, red flags went up. Word circulated among the draft gurus and NFL insiders that Browns coach Chris Palmer came away from the workout with questions about Couch's arm strength. They said he didn't like how high Couch was holding the ball when he set to throw, or the grip that Hal Mumme had taught his record-setting quarterback to employ.

Hal Mumme flashes a mischievious grin at the memory.

"Yeah," Mumme says. "Hatcher and I were a little afraid that we might get sued there for awhile, the way that guy (Palmer) was talking. I dunno. All I know is, he played well for us. Let's see what he'll do for them."

The sarcasm was intended. Hatcher is Chris Hatcher, quarterbacks coach at Kentucky and a former Division II Player of the Year when he was Mumme's quarterback at Valdosta State.

"I'll tell you," Mumme says, "if it had been me up there in Cleveland, I think I'd have been a lot more worried about who was going to be drafted two through seven than who was going to be number one."

Indeed. If Couch's throws were lacking in velocity, one had to wonder: compared to what? A bullet? A space shuttle launch?

There was suspicion that the question of arm strength was little more than an indicator that the business side of football had entered the equation. By questioning Couch's velocity and raving over the arm of quarterback Akili Smith out of Oregon, the Browns might have gained a little leverage when it came time to negotiate. After all, Couch had publicly declared how much he wanted to play for the Browns. If he meant it, he might be willing to accept a lower offer if he thought Cleveland might shun him for Smith when the negotiations got to the nitty gritty.

Whether that was the dance being played out is anybody's guess, but Elbert and Greg Couch seem convinced.

"That's just part of the game, part of the business, I think," Greg Couch says. "I don't know all the reasons why they do those things, but I'm sure part of it is to lower the value of the person. It happens every year."

"It's all about money," Elbert Couch says. "Driving the price down? Exactly right."

As for the talk about Couch's grip on the ball, Mumme says, "I was amused at first, but then I got annoyed when they started ripping our approach. It kind of hurts you in recruiting when you've got an NFL head coach rip on what you're teaching, the mechanics or the offense. That can be bad for your program."

Had Palmer ever talked to Mumme about Couch?

"No," Mumme says. "Well, we had breakfast one morning. We sat there for an hour and a half at the Marriott and we talked about horse racing, the new stadium in Cleveland, his background, my background a little bit.

"I think he asked me one question. He asked me if Tim could learn his offense. And I said, 'Well, he learned ours in a month. I mean, you guys have got all these mini-camps and everything and then six weeks of training camp. We had the month of April, then two weeks before we played Louisville, and we scored 21 points in the first quarter against a team Kentucky hadn't beaten in two years.' So I said, 'He learned ours, I imagine he can learn yours.' Then I said, 'How many plays do you all have?" And he told me, 'We don't have plays. We have *concepts.*' And when he got to that point, he lost me."

Mumme grins as his audience breaks into laughter.

"I'm from the South. We have *plays.*"

In the NFL, concepts notwithstanding, they also have investigators. That, too, became part of the deal as Cleveland scrutinized Couch. Greg says that a former Secret Service agent was hired by the Browns and did a tour of Hyden to check on Tim's background.

"It really did surprise us," Greg says. "We expected all the scrutiny. We knew it was going to happen. It happens every year with players. But you just don't realize exactly how much they look into you."

"They critique you right down to your big toenail or somethin'," Elbert Couch says, striking a blow for the sanctity of feet. "But it's just like they did with Peyton Manning last year. Slow arm, not strong enough ... they'll find some fault to you."

So it was with the "so-so" workout. With the NFL rumor machine kicking into overdrive, Akili Smith suddenly was the hot name in the draft sweepstakes. Articles began to focus on the considerable debate inside the Browns camp as to whether Couch or Smith would be the best choice to revive the Browns. Finally, it was announced that the Browns would come to Lexington one more time, on the Sunday before the draft. This time, they would put Couch through a workout of their own, with Palmer calling the shots.

The heat was on. It looked like the make-or-break moment for Tim Couch's dreams of going No. 1.

Greg and Tim really didn't change their workout leading up to the big day. They'd go through two hours of lifting followed by two hours of throwing. That Sunday morning, a Cleveland caravan complete with the entire front office staff converged on UK's Nutter Field House. Condon and the IMG boys were shooing away the local media like security guys putting the block on paparazzi at a Liz Taylor wedding (both groups, mind you, having had lots of practice). When it was all said and done, Couch had responded. Just like he did against Highlands, Louisville and Alabama. The Browns knew this was their man.

"If the draft had been held last Saturday the Browns would have taken Smith," ESPN's Chris Mortensen said, matter of factly, moments before the selection. "I think Couch's workout last Sunday convinced Chris Palmer that, yes, he has enough arm. Because they like everything about Tim but because of the style of offense and the first workout, it was hard to project Tim as the number one pick. But clearly, that workout did a lot to convince Chris Palmer."

Couch agreed.

"After the second workout I knew they really didn't have anything else to question as far as my arm strength," Tim says. "That's why I felt so comfortable about it, because they couldn't really raise any big questions about me."

"He threw that 150th pass as hard as he threw the first one," Greg says.

Later, Palmer would reveal that, as much as testing Couch's velocity, he was testing Couch's will. He kept barking out different passes to attempt, kept him throwing to the point of exhaustion, looking as much to see if Couch would balk or show frustration or even anger in the face of the demands and the physical challenge.

The brothers had done everything in their power to make their dream come true. Now it was left in the hands of the bean counters. To seal the deal, it would take a throw and catch unlike anything the Couches had ever completed before.

Draft weekend began with a Thursday night appearance on the "David Letterman Show"—a prime example of IMG's marketing muscle. With illuminates such as Tiger Woods and Tyra Banks as IMG clients, it's relatively easy to get a booking for Tim Couch. Then, early on Friday afternoon, the day before the draft, Couch posed in a photo shoot for the top six or seven draftees and a subsequent news conference. The photos would be used as a spread for a fall edition of *Gentlemen's Quarterly* called "Why We Love Football."

While Couch kibitzed and mugged with his draft "rivals" and worked the room, Tom Condon remained locked in a hotel room, trying to work out the contract. Dave Baker was in New York to report on the draft. He asked Couch how it was going.

"Tom had a meeting today and I think he's still in the meeting, " Couch said, "but I haven't had a chance to talk with him about what was said."

"So you've obviously got to be pretty happy," Baker said. "Your talking maybe 50 million dollars and you're just letting it go?"

Couch's reply: "Yeah, you know, that's what I hired him to do—to take care of me on that end, and I'll take care of football."

What Couch didn't know at the time was that the meeting had gone about as well as Art Modell's announcement that he was going to Baltimore. The shouting match that Elbert Couch says he later learned about was apparently up and running.

Because of all the negatives associated with the Browns leaving Cleveland in the first place, the last thing new owner Al Lerner wanted was for his first pick to be a holdout. The Browns wanted the pick to sign right away—possibly as soon as the day of the draft. And the Browns let it be known that they were talking to both Couch and Akili Smith. On the day following the draft in the New York newspapers, Steinberg was blunt in his assessment that the Browns had used his client, Smith, as a way of leveraging Couch into signing a contract.

At about five o'clock on a Friday afternoon—with the weekend beckoning and the subways, trains and cabs jammed with people—things can be chaotic and overwhelming even for the people who live in Manhattan, much less for those just visiting.

But for the Couch family, that was the time when things began to crystallize. Elbert was just getting back from his walk. Tim had finished the photo shoot. They sat down to dinner with Condon and Johnson. There would be a lot more than steaks on the menu. Couch would make another kind of pass, throwing the gauntlet to Condon and telling him to run with it.

"Do whatever it takes to get me to Cleveland," Couch told Condon.

The next day, when the deed was done, Couch explained why he'd told Condon to make it happen, even if it meant a lower paycheck.

"I know Cleveland is going to be my best opportunity to be successful in this league," Couch said, "so I told him that whatever it takes, just get me there. I told him that, and he went from there."

Even so, the bargain was not struck quickly. Condon entered into yet another marathon bargaining session. All Tim could do was sleep and rest up for the biggest day of his life—wherever it took him. All Elbert could do, of course, was worry through much of the night— strikingly similar to the night in 1995 when he'd waited nervously until his son told him at 3 a.m. that he wanted to be a Wildcat.

"I was pacing," Elbert says. "I kept saying, 'When's the phone gonna ring? Is it gonna ring tonight or tomorrow?'" Tomorrow had turned into today. It was 4 a.m. Had his son made a mistake? Should he have stayed at Kentucky?

It was well into daylight before the answer came. Tim was called downstairs from his hotel room at about nine o'clock. Condon had worked out the deal. It would be a base salary of $48 million with incentives that could take the deal over the $59 million mark.

Shortly thereafter, Couch became the league's only number one pick ever to actually sign his contract *before* the selection was officially announced.

"You know, the way Tim handled the draft should be a case study in how to do it right," says Tom Leach, Kentucky's play-by-play announcer. "He said where he wanted to go and he didn't try to hold out for a couple million more. He signed a good contract immediately, so he wouldn't be a holdout and wouldn't run the risk of getting off on the wrong foot with his teammates."

Ironically, even though he knew his name would be announced as the Brown's top pick, even though the contract was signed and the uncertainty was gone, the moment still gripped him.

"I felt a lot of nervousness in my stomach, sitting back there," Couch says. "Just to hear your name called. It was such a great honor."

It was more than that, of course. It was the distant dream of a little boy finally made real.

A limousine would take Couch and his family to the airport, where they were flown to Cleveland for a news conference.

Life was suddenly limos and jet-setting and bright lights and clamor.

"Aw, that didn't impress me," Elbert Couch says. "I'd rather be in my ol' red truck, headed to my garden."

11

From Top Cat to the Dawg Pound

In the heady hours after being named a number one draft choice—or number ten, for that matter—many if not most athletes are likely to throw big parties and live it up for awhile. Not Couch. The day following the draft and the news conferences that started in New York and ended in Cleveland, he was back in Lexington.

"What did you do last night?" Dave Baker asked Couch.

"Went to O'Charley's, had some dinner and looked over the playbook—for four hours," Couch said.

The conversation was one of the few breaks Couch would take over the next several days. Preparing for life as a rookie in the NFL, he poured over a playbook that resembled in thickness a New York City telephone directory. There was a daunting, encyclopedic look to the thing. Were you supposed to study it or use it for ballast?

Couch paused long enough to videotape a statewide public service announcement on the dangers of drinking and driving—a campaign called "Pass Till You're 21." But aside from that, it was doing some lifting, throwing the ball and wading through Chris Palmer's weighty tome.

Couch prepared himself as well for the zeal he'd face in Cleveland. Much as Kentucky fans treat their basketball as religion—the tone of reverence suggesting pipe organs and long robes—Browns fans treat their football like Holy Rollers—guitars, amplifiers, tambourines and, yes, more than the occasional dog bone.

Before Modell put them in football purgatory, Cleveland fans weren't just pro-active in their passion, they were preemptive. It didn't take a threat from the opposition or a bad call from the refs to stir them to action. Ask any player or official who ventured close to the Dawg Pound end zone what it was like, and they'd tell you about the plunk on the helmet or the ping to the back, heralding another Milk Bone dog biscuit that had found its mark.

The college game is a bit more dignified, of course. No hurling of a missile, however harmless its payload, would be tolerated. But in Cleveland, where the Cuyahoga used to burn, where the winters aren't for sissies and even Martin Mull, the comedian, once dreamt of being The Toe (if you've got to ask, you're just not a Browns fan), there'd be more challenge, more expectation, more of everything. Expansion would temper the immediacy of the hopes, but not the inevitability of the demand for success. A big fish in a small pond at Kentucky, he was now more like Shamu at Sea World.

Still, if he'd gone from a glass bowl to an aquarium, Couch relished the idea that he would continue to find himself around fans who seemed as passionate about the game as he was. And make no mistake, the fervor for football at the "basketball school" always is there. It is perhaps the most remarkable aspect of Kentucky football, where fans have supported the program in droves despite the lack of consistent success.

A player from one of UK's teams in the early 1980s, talking on a Lexington radio station recently, recalled that when an 0-9-1 Kentucky team closed what would be a winless season at Tennessee in 1982, there were still between 10,000 and 15,000 UK fans who'd managed to find a way into Neyland Stadium to cheer the team. Two years later, when Kentucky beat Tennessee 17-12 in Knoxville and earned a Hall of Fame Bowl bid, the players ran to the corner of the stadium where UK fans were sitting and applauded them. They'd remembered 1982.

With Couch and Mumme, they finally had something to go bonkers over again—as evidenced by the 40,000 Kentucky fans who made their way to Tampa for the Outback Bowl. Asked by WHIO-TV's Mike Hartsok if Kentucky fans and Browns fans were the same in that regard, Couch nodded an affirmative.

"It's really similar," Couch said. "Kentucky has crazy fans in both football and basketball, and Cleveland is pretty much the same way."

When Couch instructed his agent not to get in an endless haggle over his contract, one of the reasons was his realization that prima donnas are rarely welcomed with open arms by teammates, even if they do have control of the offense in their hands.

"Anytime you hold out, I think it kind of ruins relationships with your teammates," Couch said shortly after his selection. "I just wanted to come in and be one of the guys. So I'm glad we got things over with and I can come in and just concentrate on playing football."

He is one of the guys, and yet he's "The Man." Cleveland had brought in veteran Ty Detmer to quarterback the team so they could bring Couch along as slowly as necessity required. Not so slow, however, was the change in Tim Couch's financial life.

"It seems almost incomprehensible at this point," he said shortly before the draft in April. "I've got about $200 in my bank account in college, and all of a sudden I've got so many opportunities ahead of me that it's just overwhelming at times. But the fact is, they pay you to win games in this league—and with that comes a lot of pressure."

NFL rules allow you to sign a player and almost immediately have him working out in mini-camps. And so, the day after signing, there was Couch, cramming like it was final exam week with a playbook for company. Recall that Palmer's only question to Mumme had been whether he thought Couch could learn his offense. Might as well ask a bull whether it was capable of getting its game face on when a red cape was waved.

As the camp began, Couch would spend most every idle hour absorbing the playbook's contents and viewing tapes. And while it's true that at Kentucky, Mumme didn't have a playbook per se, when Couch began to talk about how Mumme's offense was "kinda like drawing up half the plays in dirt on the sidelines," a lot of media seemed to take the comment literally.

Mumme's basic offense, it is said, consists of only 15 or so plays—but in that system there are many variations. The trick isn't in its complexity, but rather in its precision, and the multiple formations from which the same patterns emerge. Mumme is a popular lecturer on the coaching classroom circuit. When last spotted, he was not seen putting his peers in a sandbox to draw up pass routes. What he *does* do is have each player bring their own notebook, and diagram the plays that he draws up on the board. "If you look at the notebooks of our quarterbacks, you're probably going to see a lot of involved stuff," Mumme said. "But if you check one of our linemen's, it's probably going to be a few chicken scratches and swirls." Why did he prefer having the players take their own notes? As a student in college, Mumme found he learned far more from the notes he took than the textbook he had to read. You tended to retain more.

Is it true that Mumme will cook up some new plays each week and might even dare to try something funky in the middle of a game if he sees a defensive weakness? You bet. Is it driving most every Southeastern Conference defense nuts trying to figure out how to stop it? You bet.

With his background as the Steelers defensive coordinator and his firsthand experience of Couch as coach at Vandy, Woody Widenhofer downplays the notion that Mumme's offense doesn't prepare a quarterback for the NFL.

"When anyone has the opportunity to throw the ball 40 or 50 or 60 times a game in a competitive league like the SEC, that's got to prepare you a little bit," Widenhofer says. "There's always a lot of reads involved and things like that in such an offense. And Couch just has so much natural ability and talent. He's just a great pure athlete, along with his ability as a leader and his poise and his ability to throw the ball. He should be as good as anybody who's ever played in the league."

Bill Curry, meanwhile, thinks the biggest challenge Couch faces is not mastering a playbook or getting used to stepping up in class in the talent-laden NFL. No, it's the obvious one: having to play on an expansion team.

"I have seen great young quarterbacks on bad teams too many times," Curry says. "I think of Archie Manning, I think of Dan Pastorini in the early years. Now, Houston came along and got good. They got some linemen to help Dan and they got Earl Campbell and Bum Phillips, so they became a playoff team while Dan was there—but I was his center in his second year and he was a very beat up, very frustrated youngster. And I got hurt and there wasn't much we could do to help him. We were just a terrible team.

"Cleveland's going to go through some of that. I just hope they get the people around Tim quickly that will allow them to compete. I think the difference in today's football will help. I don't think what happened to Archie and Pastorini will happen to Tim because I think free agency will help them get the horses. And I think Tim's presence is going to have a synergistic effect on the organization. There'll be pressure to surround him with the right kind of people, at least by the second or third year, so he just doesn't take a pounding.

"I felt so bad for Peyton Manning last year, because he really didn't have a chance. I don't want to see that happen to Tim."

As for Couch adjusting to a more complex offense, there's something else to consider. The fact is, a pro team's playbook is pretty much a formidable piece of x-and-o prose for any rookie quarterback. Mumme's offense might seem more like improvisational jazz compared to a pro team's penchant for the football equivalent of orchestral sheet music, but Couch was not alone in facing its complexity. There was a boatload of new quarterbacking talent entering the league, all of them facing the same difficult learning process.

It had been 28 years since the draft had quarterbacks go 1-2-3, but that's what happened in 1999—Couch to the Browns, Donovan McNabb of Syracuse to Philadelphia and Smith to Cincinnati. The only other time it's happened was in 1971, when Jim Plunkett, Manning and Pastorini were the top three choices.

Add to the 1999 draft the fact that Cade McNown was a high pick by Chicago and Daunte Culpepper was quickly gobbled up by Minnesota, and it was clear that this was no ordinary group of incoming quarterbacks—with Couch, the only collegiate junior among them, nevertheless gaining seniority in the order of the selections.

"Is This the Best Quarterback Class Since '83?" asked the headline on the cover of the April 19, 1999 issue of *Sports Illustrated* that preceded the actual draft. There seems little doubt that it will be. An NFL-record six quarterbacks went in the first round in 1983: John Elway, Dan Marino, Todd Blackledge, Jim Kelly, Tony Eason and Ken O'Brien.

Who will be the cream of this crop? Only time will tell, of course, but Couch shows all the signs of justifying Cleveland's faith in him.

As the mini-camps continued and Couch began to feel more comfortable with learning the offense and adjusting to the increased speed of the game, his performance began to impress Palmer. So did his honesty. Leonard Shapiro of the *Washington Post* wrote how Palmer grew enamored of Couch when, after throwing to the wrong receiver and asked by Palmer why, Couch simply said, "Coach, I forgot the play." "I thought that was great," Palmer told Shaprio. "That's the kind of kid he is. And he's only going to get better."

By August 9, he was better than any Cleveland fan, writer or coach could have hoped.

It was a Monday morning when the lovefest began. The game wouldn't be played until that night, but by midmorning thousands of Browns fans had congregated around Fawcett Stadium in Canton. Cleveland was ready to make its reappearance in the NFL. If it was a big deal on every radio and television station in Ohio that day—and it was, leading the newscasts—it loomed large in the national football psyche as well. ABC had moved the Hall of Fame game from its traditional Saturday afternoon spot to prime time.

Cleveland would be playing the Dallas Cowboys, though the opponent hardly mattered. The news was that Cleveland would be *playing*. For Browns fans, it was as if they were about to get their first drink of water in three years. They gulped it all in, the sense of celebration and anticipation and excitement that started as a constant buzz that morning escalating to electric glee when, some 10 hours later, the Browns came onto the field.

It was quite a pressurized stage for a rookie quarterback to make his debut, but for Couch it all had a familiar, comfortable feel.

Fawcett Stadium is a high school facility—albeit a big one—right in the middle of Canton. As you drove off the interstate exit, you joined the long line of cars on the city street, knowing they were all headed to the same special place. A record crowd of 25,000 had turned out—much as an overflow crowd had filled the stands and spilled over onto the grass in Lexington that August night of 1995, four years earlier, when Couch had had to prove himself in the game against Highlands.

It had a Leslie County Friday Night feel to it, too. Sure enough, on a grassy hillside overlooking the stadium, you could see smoke floating upward from charcoal grills. You had to wonder if maybe Elbert Couch hadn't turned chef again. Maybe he was up there forming another Quarterback Club.

From one end of the complex to the other, a good-sized sprinkle of people wore jerseys that said "COUCH" above the number 2. It might not be Hyden, but it was close.

"It's kind of a little different atmosphere than I had imagined for my first pro game," Couch said afterward. "It did remind you of a high school game, but you look across and you've got the Dallas Cowboys on the other side of the ball, so it was exciting."

So was Couch. On his very first play from scrimmage in the second quarter, he went deep and came within a hair of connecting. He then completed nine straight passes, one of them for a touchdown. It was a pattern right down the left hash mark from 24 yards out to Kevin Johnson, who made a fingertip catch on the dead run in the end zone. If the atmosphere surrounding Fawcett Stadium smacked of *deja vu*, so had this pass. Couch's very first touchdown pass at Kentucky, the 20-yard throw to Issac Curtis Jr., had been a virtual carbon copy, save for it coming in the right side of the end zone.

Perhaps more important than the arm he displayed that night was the crispness of the offense when he came in. The Browns seemed more alive, more intent, more seamless in their execution. Couch, of all people, knows it takes more than just throwing to get your teammates to go to war for you. And when they saw him scrambling for a first down, or getting up quickly after Nyguen rocked his world, or dropping his head and slamming into Nyguen later in the game as he tried for an extra yard near the goal line … when they saw all that, they were witnessing what virtually every player who has been a teammate of Couch has experienced.

"He's just a natural born winner," James Whalen says, "and those don't come along every day. When I first came to Kentucky as a walk-on, I thought, 'Well, I'll just play some special teams and have some fun.' But then I started playing with Tim in there, and he makes you greedy. You want more. So I found myself saying, 'OK, I'd like to play a little bit more,' and then, 'OK, I want to be a starter.' You keep growing. And it's that attitude I think that Tim has. Being a leader, he makes you want more for yourself and for your team."

When the game ended, Cleveland a giddy 20-17 winner in overtime, Couch had thrown for 137 yards on 11 of 17 passes. Wrote Terry Pluto of the *Akron Beacon-Journal*:

"So much for scouting reports. So much for Tim Couch being the nervous kid, the 22-year-old who barely needs to shave and doesn't know how to read a playbook." The headline to Pluto's column: "Just admit it, Couch looks like a winner."

"I think he's going to be the real deal", said no less an Ohio football icon than Chris Spielman. "I liked his composure as much as anything. He sat back there. He's got to learn to go down, though. You can't have $50 million taking shots like that, but he's going to be a good player for a long time, and he's going to provide a lot of excitement for Browns fans."

It was excitement already being felt by other Browns players as well—defensive lineman Jerry Ball, a 13-year NFL veteran, among them.

"Whooo! Man, he got it!" Ball gushed. "I was very impressed with him. I think that with a little more time, you guys are gonna see something special in this league. Tim Couch is a pro quarterback."

To Steve Doerschuk of Canton's newspaper, *The Repository*, Ball also noted: "Most rookie quarterbacks don't have the guts to change a play. Couch did it the first time he stepped on the field. The kid is a natural."

"I've still got a long way to go," Couch said, "but this was a good building block."

Palmer would say a couple of days later that the hope was to have Couch "up and running" by the middle of the regular season, "but I'm not so sure," he told reporters, "that he isn't on a faster track than that."

It is the only track Tim Couch knows.

"He's always done that," Elbert Couch says. "He's always been expected to be the best since he was in the third or fourth grade, and that was when he was playing against sixth- and seventh-graders. Then when he got in the sixth grade, he was expected to be better than a high school player. And when he got to be a senior in high school, he was supposed to be better than, I guess, fifty per cent of the college players. I never put any expectations on him, but people around him always expected him to do well."

Now it's Cleveland's turn. Couch wouldn't have it any other way.

"Of course, I'm going to say this because I'm his brother," Greg Couch says, "but I mean this: I think he can be the best that's ever played. I think he was the best in high school to that point. I think he was the best in college his last year. I think he'll continue to do that at the next level—just because I think he's got as much or more talent than anybody, and he *absolutely* outworks everybody. He knows what he wants, he knows where he wants to get and he knows what it takes to get there."

12

Talkin' Tim: An Oral History

In the still young but already remarkable career of Tim Couch, there are countless moments that serve to define him as a player and a person. Here, a number of people—from media representatives to coaches to teammates, friends and family—recall some of their favorites.

I'll always remember a phone conversation I had with Leslie County coach Mike Whitaker early in the 1993 season. He was telling me about a sophomore quarterback he had who was racking up big passing yardage, and how the 16-year-old kid had all the tools of a big-time prospect, and how he was already the best quarterback in the state. I said something polite in response—I had heard this kind of claim from a hundred other coaches over the years—but Whitaker persisted.

"When I say he's the best quarterback in the state, I mean high school or college," Whitaker said. "He's better than Pookie Jones (at Kentucky) or Jeff Brohm (at the University of Louisville) right now. If he picks the right college, he'll be playing on Sundays (in the NFL) someday."

I can't recall what I said next, but again I tried to disguise my skepticism. Anyway, I put Whitaker's comments in the newspaper, prompting just about everybody outside of Hyden to question the coach's sanity. How could this kid from the mountains named Tim Couch, only a sophomore, be that good?
—*Lexington Herald-Leader sportswriter Mike Fields*

It was the day after Thanksgiving in 1994, Couch's junior year. Mark Coomes and I drove to Hyden to see Couch in a state playoff game. We were late. We'd missed the Daniel Boone Parkway and ended up on one of those serpentine roads where you go 10 miles an hour, reeling back and forth. We nearly died about 15 times.

So we finally get there in the middle of the first quarter. We pull up and the stadium is in a valley, and there's this creek and you've got to cross a bridge or something to get to it. So we park a long ways away from the stadium. There's 11,000 people at this little stadium. We're not there yet, but you can see Couch on the field. And it's the first time I've ever seen him, and right then he throws this ball that's unbelievable. Perfect motion. Perfect action. Throws this ball and this little scrawny receiver comes into the end zone and it's right there. Thirty-five yards or something. Perfect. On the money. We both looked at each other and said, "Wow." It was like, "Whoa! We're here for the right reason."

We finally get to the pressbox and stand on top of it to watch. It's freezing cold, but every pass was like that.

Nobody had to stretch or move or dive to catch his passes. And you had to figure, considering the athletic challenges of those receivers, that's probably where he *had* to throw it. And that's kind of Couch. Wherever he needs to put it, he can put it there.

—*Louisville Courier-Journal sports columnist Pat Forde*

From the first time I ever saw Tim, he was the best quarterback I had ever seen. I think that was after his sophomore year in high school. I had heard about him, but I heard about a lot of highly touted quarterbacks. But after just a day at our camp it was very clear that he was beyond anything I had ever seen. Probably the best at any position I'd ever seen. There was an intuitive sense to him, and the clear mark of somebody destined to do something real special— and that it was easy for him to do it.

—*Former UK coach and ESPN analyst Bill Curry*

The first time I saw him, he was a sophomore. The thing that stands out, even more than the game, was the warm-up. Word had begun to spread that Couch was the real deal. I don't even remember who Leslie County was playing, but it was packed. And I remember going up to this crowded little press box and looking down and seeing him throw balls to his receivers in the pre-game. Every one was a perfect spiral, exactly on target—30, 40 yards downfield. What made it doubly impressive was that, for the most part, all of them were being caught. And even the ones that weren't were pretty passes to watch. I was so impressed by him before the game even started.

It's a great atmosphere down there, with the Friday night lights and the mountains right around you. You're sort of in a little valley of football.

—*Lexington Herald-Leader sportswriter Mark Maloney*

I don't think I'll ever forget the first time I found out how good Couch was. It came before I ever laid eyes on him. I was a high school beat writer for the *Anderson News* in Lawrenceburg. Anderson County never played Leslie County when Couch was in high school. But in Couch's senior year, Leslie County was playing Woodford County the week before Anderson would play Woodford. Anderson and Woodford are only about ten miles apart, and at the time their game was probably the biggest non-district game on either schedule.

I was covering Anderson's away game that night. Because I wasn't on a daily deadline, Anderson's coach, Anthony Hatchell, suggested we drive back to the school in Lawrenceburg to do the post-game interview. When we pulled up to the field house, Derek Shouse and Brian Klink—the two assistants he'd sent to scout Woodford County—were already there.

Shouse spoke first. He was, after all, supposed to give Hatchell his impressions of Woodford County, their big rival. Instead, his first words were: "Tim Couch is unbelievable." Klink, who was kind of quiet, just sat there, shaking his head in exaggerated fashion, as if he too couldn't quite fathom what he'd witnessed.

I had heard of Couch and read about him, but didn't believe anyone could be *that* good. In fact, I sort of dismissed it. On Monday, I stopped by Hatchell's office for the Woodford scouting report to put in the paper. Hatchell was watching film of the Woodford-Leslie game and he said,

"John, you cannot believe this kid. Sit down here and watch this." I thought he was referring to a Woodford County player who was pretty good, so I kept looking for him.

"No!" Hatchell finally said. "I mean Couch! Watch him. You will never see a better football player in Kentucky."
—*Anderson News sportswriter John Herndon*

One of the unusual things came in a game at Woodford County. Afterward, I was going up to the locker room when I see what seems like at least half the Woodford County team asking Couch for his autograph. That's the first time I ever saw opponents going over to get the autograph of the star player from the other team. He handled it like he was already in college.

I also saw him at a Cincinnati Bengals-Miami Dolphins game his senior year. Larry Seiple, a former Kentucky and Dolphin player, had set it up so Tim could meet Dan Marino after the game. Marino is a pretty imposing figure physically, and here's Couch, still in high school, standing next to him, and there really wasn't a lot of difference between the two. I'm sure there was weight-wise, but they were almost the same height, and they both had that aura about them.

Marino told him, "I hope I'm still playing when you get in the league." —*Mark Maloney*

I remember broadcasting the Thoroughbred Bowl in Tim's senior year. I had heard all the stories and seen him on highlights, but I'd never seen him in person. Real early, he made this throw that was the equivalent of a shortstop in baseball making the throw from deep in the hole. He was on the right hash mark and threw a long out pattern all the way across to the other sideline. He hit the guy perfect, just as he was going out of bounds. It went for about 30 yards. He makes that throw, and I remember thinking, "This guy is the real thing." And he looked the part of a quarterback—size and presence. As you got to know him, you saw how confident he was and how much leadership he had.

You know, my first season as Kentucky's announcer was Tim's first season in the Air Raid. People have been very nice to me with compliments on my call of the games, but there's luck involved, too. I mean, if I sounded exciting it's partly because Tim Couch made things so exciting. He gave me the chance to say "Touchdown, Kentucky!" a *lot* of times.

—*UK radio network play-by-play announcer Tom Leach*

After a press-hyped national letter of intent signing at Couch's high school, the Leslie County booster club was selling 8x10 color glossies of Tim throwing the national record-breaking touchdown pass. Individual prints sold for $10. It was then that the Tim Couch merchandise machine began. Even though I'm old enough to be his father, I couldn't resist buying one of the pictures and getting his autograph.   —*WLEX-TV sports director Gary Johnson*

I felt like I saw the field well, but that's one thing that separates Tim from anybody else I've ever seen. He's just got an *x* quality that I don't think you can teach. He sees things, and it's just natural. He's big, he's mobile, he can throw the ball—but the thing that separates him, I would think, would be his composure, just the way he sees the field and his ability to stay calm when everything's coming at him, and still find the right guy. —*Greg Couch*

Tim has that rare quality—and it's all about anticipation. The ball is gone before the receiver makes his break. Great quarterbacks must have the gift to throw the ball before it's apparent that there's a good chance for a completion—and then, they may not even be able to tell you *why* they did it.

The next part of that is intuition, an intuitive feel for the game. And that includes peripheral vision, some of what announcers love to call a "sixth sense." Tim also knows where the defensive end is that's getting ready to drive a Ridell through his earhole. He really does. OK, so he's got all this stuff. And he seems to have had it from the time he was just a little boy. And he definitely had it from the time he was a sophomore in high school, because I saw it. Plus, he was a likable sort, a good person. I mean, he just had everything you've ever looked for. —*Bill Curry*

My involvement with Tim was mainly his freshman year in 1996, when Uzelac and Curry didn't play him. As long as I've been writing, I've never really criticized a coach for much of anything except cheating. This was the first time I really got on a coach for what I considered to be incompetence.

You know, Kentucky just never had a kid like this. And why they didn't recognize that and see that … I just thought it was criminal to put him in that option attack. So, I wrote some stuff about that.

The thing that always really impressed me about Couch is that he's just always had this incredible poise about him. I always thought Tim seemed to be a lot older than he really is. I don't think any athlete in Kentucky's history, including basketball players, ever had the kind of adulation and expectations that surrounded him, and yet he just always handled it in a very mature way. And I think they're finding that out now in Cleveland.

And for a kid from the mountains to succeed in this way—you know, sometimes people tend to think they're a little bit backward socially in some ways, that they've lived their whole lives in the mountains and when they make the adjustment it's sometimes hard for them to adapt to a new climate. But Tim was just, from day one, a very poised, mature guy.

And he's just so unruffled. It was like he was probably the least guy of all surprised by the success he had at Kentucky. Thank God they did get Mumme and his system in at the time. I just think Tim's a guy who Kentuckians ought to really be proud of, coming from where he did and the way he's handled it. You talk about a role model in this day and time; he's one of them.

—Lexington Herald-Leader and Sports Illustrated writer Billy Reed

In the '96 season opener against Louisville, he threw a beautiful pass to Isaac Curtis for a touchdown, I was awestruck. Kentucky quarterbacks didn't make those kind of passes. And yet, Billy Jack Haskins was still the starter. I loved Haskins. I thought he was as responsible for Kentucky's four wins in 1995 as anyone. But in talking with high school coaches, I kept hearing, "Couch is as good a player as they will ever get, and look what they're doing with him." Or, "Haskins is a good player, tough kid. He'll make a nice high school or college coach some day. But Couch will be playing on Sundays—*if* Uzelac doesn't mess him up."

—*John Herndon*

Paul Hornung played with Bill Curry for the Packers, and in Couch's senior year in high school, Hornung came up from his Louisville home and addressed the banquet. Naturally, although he went to Notre Dame, he was encouraging Couch to come to Kentucky. At some point while there he visited Couch's home and went into Tim's room. Afterward, he said, "I came back and I told Bill, 'There's nothing in there but blue. I don't think you have anything to worry about.'"

As much as he liked Curry, Paul was one of the first ones (to criticize) when he found out they were going to run an option offense and not play Tim. Hornung was very outspoken about that. He's always said that Tim has the potential to be another John Elway. He just thinks that in terms of his ability to throw the ball, his ability to lead and his ability to scramble a little bit … he's always compared him to Elway.

—*Billy Reed*

Throughout that season, Tim was a jewel. He never put the coaching staff in a bind, although he had many chances publicly because he was constantly asked about it. He just did his job the best he could. The thing I'll always be grateful to Tim for is that he didn't leave Kentucky.

Even with the coaching change, there was no guarantee he'd stay. Let's face it. Had we gone out and hired somebody who's a known quarterback coach and so on—say, a Mike Shannahan—that's an easy decision for Tim to make. But when you hire Hal Mumme from Valdosta State and you've got all the people telling him that he ought to be going to Tennessee or he ought to be going here or there ... I think for Tim to have the kind of confidence he had in us was extraordinary.

Part of it was driven by the fact that he genuinely loves this place. I mean, that's the key thing that a lot of people didn't understand about Tim from day one. You have to understand Eastern Kentucky folks, and how they feel about this university to really have an understanding of it. And I understand it because I've been around it so long. Like Phil Cox (a basketball player from the mountains), for example. Phil was great for Vanderbilt, but, you know, he would have killed to play in this program. So I had a good understanding of that. But to me, what Tim did was a real show of strength, that he believed enough and wanted to be here enough that he just hung in there with us.

I think Tim did for this program what Leon Douglas did for the Alabama basketball program when I coached there. I know the breakthrough we had at Alabama was Leon Douglas, who was from Alabama, making the decision to play for us. That just put the stamp on it: "Yeah, these people are really serious. Here's one of the most highly recruited players in the country."

And that's what Tim's coming here did. You know, Tim is the first player of his stature to stay in state. I mean, you lose a Hornung to Notre Dame and you lose this guy there, but then you get someone like Tim who is so visible as a high school recruit to come into your program. And when you do, it's critical that he succeed. Coming here is one thing. But kind of washing through and being ordinary can hurt the program.

For Tim to have the kind of two-year career that he had—which is really what it turned out to be—and then be the number one draft choice in the country, and also be the kind of role model that he was—all that success validates that he chose Kentucky. And it's not just what he did on the field. I mean, you see every youngster still wearing those No. 2 shirts. He was a real role model, in every way.

—*UK athletics director C.M. Newton*

We thought we might still wind up getting Tim. I mean, I knew there were some bad rumors, people calling me who were close to the situation, telling me that he wasn't happy and he might be leaving. And then, if you'll remember, during that period my name got mentioned as a candidate for the coaching position at Kentucky. I had actually interviewed. So I knew I had an opportunity going in, that if I had the opportunity to get this job, it would be to coach Tim Couch. It was really an unusual time. But everything has a reason for working out like it does, and it worked out for the best for everybody concerned.

—*Former Tennessee assistant and current Ole Miss coach David Cutcliffe*

One of the few times I could actually hear what Couch was saying to his teammates after a touchdown—because generally the crowd was so loud I couldn't hear, but I stuck my head in there this time—was in the middle of the upset win over Alabama in 1997. I watched him animatedly talking to the rest of the offense. It was almost as if he wanted to will them to a victory. And he said, "To be a champion, it's got to *burn* inside of you! You've got to want it!"

They had all sat down in those chairs for the offensive unit after they'd reconnoitered with Hal Mumme following the touchdown, and they were geeked. They just kept yelling, "We can do it, we can do it!"

—*UK radio network sideline announcer Dick Gabriel*

Tim has the ability to be extremely confident without being cocky. He has a better combination of this than anybody I've ever met. When he goes out there on the field, he believes that he's going to throw a bunch of touchdown passes and he's going to lead his team to victory—and yet, he's not cocky about that. He knows very well that it might go in exactly the opposite direction.

At Kentucky, he had a remarkable humility about him in that sense. He was extremely confident he was going to succeed. He absolutely believes he's going to succeed in everything he does, and yet it's not cockiness. That's a marvelous personality trait. And to this day, I'm still not sure how he achieved it. I don't know how you get that balance. More than anything else, that's what I marveled at.

—*UK media relations director Tony Neely*

I thought the fact he was carrying the weight of the program on his shoulders most of the time he was playing was pretty significant. He's such a mild interview, and yet the expectations of Kentucky fans and of the University, and certainly of Coach Mumme, the validation of hiring him … in reality it boiled down to how Couch played week in and week out.

Plays that stood out? The two out patterns he threw to Yeast at LSU. The out pattern is very difficult to throw. As a junior against Mississippi State, he hit the long ball and they called it back for holding, I think.

The long ball was tough, because everybody always questioned that. And yet, nobody ever really gave him the long ball. I thought that was the most significant thing. More than the fact he didn't make the long ball throws was that the defenses didn't give it to him because they were afraid of it. I always thought he had an arm. I think people label you so much and they only look at it from one side. Tim had to work for it. They wanted to lay deep on him and keep everything in front. And if you're not given it, why go for it? You're not going to get it anyhow if they're playing too deep all the time. I thought that was the ultimate respect for his arm, rather than the other way around, with people concluding that he couldn't throw it.

—*UK radio color announcer Jeff Van Note*

You never really knew Tim was around. I mean, he never asked for anything. Some players want new this, new that—but with Tim, we'd have to go in and almost force him to change the bottom of his cleats. He never asked for anything—maybe a pair of socks if the ones he was wearing had holes in them. But they had to have holes in them first. The only thing that he was concerned about were the sleeves on his game jersey, to have them cut open to make sure he was able to throw.

Over the years, the great ones? They never ask for anything. They know what they want. They're focused. They know that socks don't make it, shoes don't make it. It's what's inside that does. And I think that was Tim's focus the whole time, to do what he wound up doing, become the number one draft choice.

I remember when he was on his recruiting visit. He just stayed in the equipment room the whole time, just hung out with the managers. He just sat in here and watched TV with us. He was very unassuming. Never big time—the type guy you can cut up and say just about anything with. Some people, I guess, look at him now as Tim Couch, the millionaire, the number one draft pick. But Tim's just Tim. To us, he's Tim.

That's why his teammates were so loyal to him. He was one of them. He wasn't a three-piece suit guy. He's just an ol' country boy. That's the biggest thing. He's just an ol' country boy and everybody knew that. To me, there's an Eastern Kentucky love. There's something about a player from Eastern Kentucky that's so much different from any other part of the state. You can go back to the Ritchie Farmer era in basketball—how everybody was just wild over him. And that's just the type person Tim is, too—very unassuming.

I'll tell you a story. They had the NFL draft so, boom, Tim signs his contract – boom, boom, boom—for whatever millions of dollars that Saturday. And I guess it was Monday, at about 11:30, and my equipment room door opens up. Tim and his brother Greg come in, carrying their Arby's sandwiches. Just sat down on the couch and ate lunch before workouts, y'know? No talk about $60 million and blah, blah, blah. Just the normal Tim.

—*UK equipment manager Tom Kalinowski*

He's done pretty good. He's not going out and wasting money and everything. He got himself a car and a house, and that's pretty much it. —*Greg Couch*

I did get the chance to interview Couch on two separate occasions. Unlike so many, he didn't exhibit a false humility. He was confident, no doubt about that, but he prefaced answers with "Yes, sir" and "No, sir." I did one interview with him just before the 1998 season. By this time, of course, he was already national news, and here I was, a reporter for a weekly newspaper. The day I talked to him, several major papers were on the schedule, too. I'm sure that even though I tried to ask different questions, many of them he had heard a million times before. Yet he answered all of them as if he'd heard them for the first time. Then I said, "Does it bother you that you're grabbing all the headlines and the rest of the team is kind of forgotten?" He said, "Sometimes I *do* get tired of hearing about myself."

Later, I talked with offensive line coach Guy Morriss and asked him about the linemen's relationship with Couch. He crossed his fingers and said, "They're like this. If Tim were a jerk, they probably wouldn't play so hard for him."

—*John Herndon*

I got a phone call from a guy one night. Sounded like he was a different nationality, Arabic or something. He said he was an agent and wanted to ask about Tim Couch because the draft was coming up. And I said, "Well, you know, we really can't say anything about it. It's against the rules. Call our people."

But the guy just wouldn't let me get off the phone. I'm thinking, "I don't want to be rude to this guy." But after awhile I figured somebody's playing a joke on me, so I got very blunt, very rude and hung up.

Well, the guy calls me back, and this got me to thinking, "Golly, maybe this is somebody real." He's giving me his number, his certification number, everything. Tells me his name, where his offices are, so I thought, "Now I've pissed him off. This isn't good."

So I say, "I'm sorry, I didn't mean to be rude. I thought somebody was playing a joke on me." And as I began telling him again that I really couldn't tell him anything, the person just breaks out laughing.

It was Tim. He had a voice-thrower, one of those little machines that changes your voice. And he had a house full of people just dying laughing in the background. Needless to say, this brought on a lot of phone wars.
—*Kentucky quarterback Dusty Bonner, Couch's successor*

He used to sing country music all the time in practice. He'd sing that song, "Dixieland Delight" by Alabama. One of the lines goes, "Rolling down the backwoods of Tennessee byways, sweet soft Southern breeze…" but he'd always change it. He'd sing, "Rolling down the backwoods of Leslie County byways…"

A bunch of the players would join him and sing George Strait's "Call Me the Fireman" a lot, too. And he'd sing Hank Williams' "A Country Boy Can Survive." He'd just sing it all the time. Of course, he'd change that, too. It was "A Leslie County Boy Can Survive." —*UK student manager Jodi Gillespie*

The funniest thing Tim did? Well, he's a hundred percent country. He listens to Hank Williams, Jr., and David Allen Coe and people like that. And you'd hear him on the bus. But one time some other players in the back of the bus are playing Master P, who sort of grunts a lot, and singing rap music, and they're doing this and they're doing that. Suddenly one of them shouts out, "Hey Tim, rap for us!" And Tim's like, *Sheeeeeeit, what are you talkin' about?* Then he lets out with this loud groan, kind of like "UNNNNNNNNNNGH!" And then he turns to them and says, "That's all you get." I was rolling over in the aisle.

Tim's a character. If I could speculate, his favorite vacation would probably be sitting by a pond somewhere fishing and maybe drinking a cold beer. That's probably Tim's favorite place in the world. He's a lot like (Jeff) Snedegar. He's got that fiery country boy attitude. And that's the way he lives his life. He plays football the way he lives his life.   *—UK tight end James Whalen*

Sometimes he'd sing *in the huddle.* Some ol' crazy stuff—some ol' crazy country music, and we'd look at him all silly. He'd do it all the time.
                    —UK wide receiver Craig Yeast

Tim was very impressive from his first day here, because he was the most media-ready freshman with whom I'd ever dealt. Of course, he'd been through it. Basically, his junior year in high school was when the national media started paying attention to him, so he'd been through two years of extensive media. But I marveled at how easy it was for him. He never struggled through interviews—and I could catch him at any point, any time, and he'd do a great interview just like that.

I always told people, I could wake Tim at 2 o'clock in the morning, shine a light in his face, get him out of bed and tell him it was a CBS live national interview, and he'd do it without a hitch—because that's just how ready he was. Tim's personality was such that the guy you saw on the camera was the same guy off. He didn't go into interview mode or anything like that. What you saw is what you got.

—*Tony Neely*

What pisses me off about people's perception of Tim is the stereotype of being just a country hick from Hyden. What I found was that he was one of the smartest athletes I've ever come across.

Two stories: It's 1997, playing South Carolina on the road, and Kentucky blows it. South Carolina is feeling really crappy about themselves, and there's turmoil around the coaching staff. It was the kind of game where Kentucky should have won by three touchdowns. They'd jumped ahead 14-0 and had a chance to demoralize them.

But Tim doesn't have a good game. And I forget which interception it was, but one really hurt. Afterward, I'm one of about eight guys around him. "Hey, Tim, what were you thinking about when you threw the interception?" "How much longer did you think about the interception?" And he said, "I forgot about it right away." I asked why, and Tim said, "Because I'm the quarterback, and I have to have the shortest memory on the team. If I go back in the huddle and I'm upset, even if I don't say anything and the guys see it, it affects everybody else. If I show it, then everybody's going to perform poorly. So I have to have the shortest memory."

The second thing was outside the TV station about two weeks before he was going to be a freshman. He showed up to do some public service announcement on a walk to raise money for charity, so I grabbed him for an interview.

He'd just been in *USA Today* within the last couple of weeks in an article about his high school career.

Normally, of course, when you ask a question you usually have an idea what kind of answer you're going to get, but his absolutely blew me away. I said, "Tim, why'd you break all these records." And he said, "Because I set goals." Seventeen years old. "Where did you learn to set goals?" I figured he'd say that he learned how in school. He didn't. He said he learned in summer football camps. He said, "Coaches always told me to set goals, so I figured, what the heck. I tried it, it worked, so I do it all the time." And then he said, "Every year I've played football since, I've set goals and I've made every single one of them. So I'll set goals for next year because I want to be directed."

I have found Tim Couch to be probably better mentally than physically, and I don't think a lot of people understand that because of the twang of his voice.

—WLEX-TV sports reporter and WLXG radio talk show host Alan Cutler

He's a goal setter and he visualizes things. And it seems like they always come true.　　　　*—Greg Couch*

We did an interview once with Landry Collet, a city policeman now in Hyden (and a high school teammate of Couch), and he said that when Tim was 11 years old, he had a little notebook he carried around with him. Tim showed him the notebook, and in it he'd written down some goals. One of them was to be the number one pick in the NFL draft someday.　　　*—WYMT-TV sports reporter John Lewis*

My best memory of Couch actually comes from his fiance, Sarah Gilliam. She told me that after the Outback Bowl against Penn State, when the couple was watching a videotape of the game, one particular first down scramble by Tim stood out so much that they'd rewind the tape over and over to watch it. It was the one when Tim lowered his head and collided with three Penn State players, including Lavar Arrington. It was a huge hit, but he sprang up quickly and gave an enthusiastic first down signal with his right arm. Sarah said she and Tim kept watching that play, laughing at how pumped up Tim had been signaling that first down.

—*Gary Johnson*

On the day Tim was ready to tell us that he was leaving Kentucky early for the NFL draft, Tony Neely said, "Tim's on his way over here. He's made his decision." And I said, "Tony, do you know?" And he said, "Well, he's leaving," as in, "of course." So I said, "Couldn't you have broken it to me a little bit more gently, Tony? Couldn't you have built up to it?"

But I knew. So Tim comes in, and he says he wants to have his press conference down at the Radisson—where he'd announced he was coming to Kentucky, too.

I called him into my office and said, "Tim, I'm going to talk to you as much as a fan right now as an assistant AD. The press conference at the Radisson. One thing. That's where you were when you announced you were coming to Kentucky, and the fans might not understand you going back there to say you're leaving." And he said, "You're kidding, you're joking." And I said, "No, I'm not joking. That's still one of the greatest moments of my sports life, seeing you down there." He said, "Aw, you're grillin' me." And I said "No, I'm not." And he says, "Well, everybody knows what I'm going to do." And I said, "No. Everyone in this state is thinking that you might stay because of your family and UK, because you love Kentucky football." And he goes, *"Really?"* I said, "Until about 20 minutes ago, I was one of those people." "Really?" he says again. I said, "Yeah."

So he decided instead to have the press conference with Hal Mumme at his side, in a conference room under Commonwealth Stadium, where he'd had all his moments of glory. It's kind of like he got back to what he thought about Kentucky football, and finally realized the impact he'd had. I think he stepped back and realized, "This is going to crush the state." *—UK assistant athletic director Rena Vicini*

As for the pros, I think the conventional wisdom says to bring him along slowly and don't throw him in there because it could damage his confidence. And yet, from the time I've been around him and in talking to people who know him, I really don't think there's much risk of that.

I'm sure he'll have his struggles. Peyton Manning did the first half of his rookie season. But Tim is so well grounded. And number two, after what happened his first year at Kentucky, with all he went through with the Uzelac system ... if that didn't shake his confidence or damage him, a few interceptions his first year in the NFL isn't going to do it. *—Tom Leach*

During Couch's first week of training camp with the Browns in Berea, Ohio, a swarm of media hovered around his locker waiting for him to get out of the shower. It gave us a chance to study the various items visible in the open locker. There was a maroon baseball cap with "LC" sewn onto the front, and other items from his high school days. It was a reminder to me that no matter how many millions he will earn or how far he was from home, Tim would keep that connection with Leslie County.   —*Gary Johnson*

We'd play paper-rock-scissors on Thursday nights before games to see who'd carry each other's bags. The funniest thing about it was, he's the Heisman Trophy candidate and all this good stuff, and he ended up carrying my bag most of the time. I'd give him heck. He beat me the first couple of times and then I just started killing him for the rest of the season. I guess I just figured him out.

I'd watch him play pool against somebody else. He'd be doing bad or the other guy was winning, and he'd just hand the guy the stick, walk down to the other end of the table like he was mad and take one of his balls and put it in the pocket when the guy couldn't see it."

He used to come over to the house and play Nintendo, the Madden game. He was terrible at it. I wasn't great, but I could beat him. And for awhile he really couldn't score a touchdown. He could go out on Saturdays and throw five or six, so that really irritated him. Well, we'd get to the fourth quarter in this computer game and I'd just be stomping him. He'd throw an interception and he'd take the game controller and just sling it down and walk out the door without saying a word. He'd call me later. Usually when he called, it'd be, "Maaaan, you're cheatin'!"

He was just so competitive. At the same time, he worked really hard and deserved everything he got. I mean, he really does. In some ways he's kind of shy, just because he's got so much attention from everybody. He doesn't want to do anything wrong to make anybody upset. He always wants to be polite, things like that. I regard him as a real good friend. He's really helped me out a lot in football. Most look at him now as Tim Couch, NFL quarterback. To me he's just Tim, you know? He's just a good ol' boy.

—*Dusty Bonner*

Me and Tim were at a restaurant in Lexington recently and a media guy who had been critical in the past came up and said, "Congratulations, Tim." When he left, I said, "Tim, that's the guy who really, really ripped you." And he said, "I love people like that, dad. I love to prove 'em wrong."

—*Elbert Couch*

Epilogue

A week before Kentucky was to open its 1999 season, Dusty Bonner stood on the field in Commonwealth Stadium following his team's dress rehearsal practice for the following Saturday's game with Louisville.

As he looked around, the evidence of Kentucky football's resurgence was everywhere. No longer were there smallish bleachers behind the end zones. Stadium expansion had bowled in both ends, the seats now reaching as high as the sideline lower decks. Perched above the new seating were large luxury skyboxes, stretching from corner to corner, the only breaks in their construction to make room for two huge new scoreboards with Diamondvision screens. Across the top section of each scoreboard, which towered nearly as high as the top of the sideline upper decks, KENTUCKY WILD-CATS was spelled out. It loomed large. The whole place loomed large.

Bonner allowed himself a smile.

"To me, it's amazing," he said.

He wasn't talking about the stadium per se. He was talking about the person who had played such an instrumental role in its metamorphosis. He was talking about Tim Couch.

"Here he is," Bonner said, "a guy who kind of turned around this program when coach Mumme came in. Everybody's excited and football's exciting. Everybody wants to be here. You look at this stadium now and it's awesome."

So is the challenge of following a legend. Bonner, a steady and determined sort, welcomes that. It's a key factor in why Mumme chose him to succeed Couch as Kentucky's quarterback. But on this day, he didn't feel the need to talk about relishing the challenge.

He wanted to talk about how special it had been to be around Tim Couch.

"Just to be able to say you were there when he played at Kentucky, you know?" Bonner said. "Just to watch him play, because he's a guy I'm sure will be in the NFL for a long time and definitely make his mark. It's neat."

It was all neat. But where had they gone, those three neat years? They were highlight reel now—relegated to history so quickly that surely someone had pressed fast forward. But the legacy was alive. Even as Couch set out to create yet another legacy in Cleveland, his impact on Kentucky football was as tangible as the vast new landscape that Commonwealth Stadium offered up.

"I guess they were making plans on this for 20 years, and they finally did it, " James Whalen says. "I think the fans here at Kentucky are probably some of the best in the nation, for the simple fact that they were selling out almost every game when they were going 2-9. I mean, are you kidding me? Who wants to come and watch a team lose? That's just dedication and loyalty from the state of Kentucky. And now it's really fun because it's not just us playing, it's everyone. We're getting to share what we've become with the people of Kentucky."

Ultimately, what Couch left was a sense that Kentucky, with a coach like Mumme in place, did indeed have the chance to make a bigger name for itself, did have a reason to stay excited. Even with him gone, even with expansion that increased stadium capacity by 10,000 seats, Kentucky recorded only the third sellout of its season ticket allotment in school history. And the sellout was completed in April of 1999, the earliest it had ever happened.

The funny thing was, there had been fans who envisioned what Couch might mean to Kentucky football long before. Rob Plenge is a UK grad who lives in Washington, New Jersey. A husband, father and business owner, he had followed Couch's high school exploits from afar. When recruiting was in its final stages, it was Plenge who wrote a letter to the editor of the fan tabloid *The Cats Pause*. It was so impassioned that the editors gave it a large headline across one page. In the December 2, 1995 issue, Plenge's letter had become virtually an article. And the headline read:

TIM COUCH CAN BE A KENTUCKY LEGEND

The open letter came just three weeks before Couch signed with Kentucky. In part, Plenge wrote: "Dream ... of Commonwealth Stadium being bowled in. Tim Couch ... could make a difference like no Kentucky athlete before."

Plenge would form a Couch Quarterback Club over the next few years. When Couch threw the first touchdown pass of his career in 1996 on this same field, Plenge had heard it from his New Jersey home, a buddy in the stands shouting the play-by-play to him over a cell phone. Later, he would bump into Couch and his father during a visit to Lexington. He would discover that, back when he'd made his plea, the letter wound up on Tim Couch's bedroom wall in Hyden.

Passion. Couch's own ignited the same in others. It's there now with Kentucky's players as well.

"I was talking to Coach Mumme about this just a couple of days ago," James Whalen had said back in June. "We're out there working out in the afternoons, just the players, and we do our pass drills. And there are so many people out there that we had to split into two groups. We were talking about that with Coach and he said, 'You know, Tim never had that problem because we couldn't get this many people out here in the summer.'

"I think it's just because people want to get better. They want to win. They've experienced a little tiny taste of what it's like to win, and they want it to grow."

In the dawgish delirium surrounding the revival of Cleveland Browns football, Couch will find kindred spirits. Few who know him, few if any who have seen his skills up close, doubt that Couch can't do for Cleveland what he did for Kentucky.

Asked who he thought might prove the better pro, Couch or Peyton Manning, Bill Curry didn't hesitate.

"I think Tim's a better athlete than Peyton," Curry said. "The fact that Peyton played in an already up-and-running sophisticated system that was suited to his talents at Tennessee was a huge advantage. And he had blue chip wide receivers who were already developed the day he walked under center.

"Manning is a great person and a great talent, but he's not the throwing talent that Tim is. Peyton had all those advantages that Tim didn't have as a freshman with us, but then he ran into that buzz saw in the NFL because everything moves up a notch, and even Peyton had to adjust. He would pass for 300 yards but he would throw three interceptions. And I'd see this dejected face coming off to the sideline, because what he really wants is the same thing Tim really wants, which is to win.

"So I just hope Tim doesn't go through that. But I think Tim's got a chance to be an even greater talent."

Hal Mumme is more succinct, but equally convinced.

"I'm sure anytime you go to the next level there are things that are going to be new and different and you've got to adjust to them," he says, "but Tim will be great, because he's got a great passion for doing it. He's going to adapt to anything they want."

Without question, part of the renaissance at Kentucky was the result of Mumme's coaching and Craig Yeast's remarkable ability not only to make the catch, but to turn short slants and flanker slip-screens into long-range touchdown sprints. The Deuce and The Trey (Yeast wore No. 3) were not only the most explosive combination in UK and Southeastern Conference history, they also were—without much argument—the two greatest players in school history at their positions.

A short while after the Browns signed him, the SEC named Couch its Male Athlete of the Year. When Couch's final season at UK was in the books, Kentucky had led the SEC in total offense for the first time in school history, averaging 534.2 yards per game. And it had set an SEC record by averaging 412.2 yards per game passing.

There's a pass in passion—which is as it should be when defining the fire that burns in Couch. It will burn in him as long as he plays the game. It will burn through the cold Novembers alongside Lake Erie. It will burn with each pass thrown, each hit taken and each touchdown scored.

There in Commonwealth Stadium, it will continue to burn as well. It is the legacy Tim Couch left for a state and a school.

Tim Couch Statistics

AWARDS & HONORS

•First-Team All-American, 1998
(Walter Camp Foundation, Football Writers Association)

•Second-Team All-American, 1998
(Associated Press, Football News)

•First-Team All-SEC, 1998
•Second-Team All-SEC, 1997

•SEC Player of the Year, 1998
•SEC Male Athlete of the Year, 1998-99
•1998 Atlanta Touchdown Club Award (presented annually since 1939 to the outstanding player in the Southeastern Conference)

SCHOOL AND CONFERENCE RECORDS HELD BY TIM COUCH

Southeastern Conference Individual Records

Career Records
Total Offensive Yards Per Game: 281.4 (1996-98)
Highest Pass Completion Percentage: 67.1 (1996-98)

Season Records
>Most Total Offensive Plays: 617 (1998)
>Most Total Offenisve Yards: 4,151 (1998)
>Most Total Offensive Yards Per Game: 377.4 (1998)
>Most Passes Attempted: 553 (1998)
>Most Completions: 400 (1998)
>Most Passing Yards: 4,275 (1998)
>Highest Pass Completion Percentage: 72.3 (1998)

University of Kentucky Records

Total Offense
Most Offensive Plays, Career
1,338 (8,160 yards), 1996-98

Most Offensive Plays, Season
617 (4,151 yards), 1998
613 (3,759 yards), 1997

Most Offensive Plays, Game
74 vs. LSU (392 yards), Nov. 1, 1997

Total Yards
Most Total Offensive Yards, Career
8,160 (1,338 plays), 1996-98

Most Total Offensive Yards, Season
4,151 (617 plays), 1998
3,759 (613 plays), 1997

Most Total Offensive Yards, Game
498 vs. Louisville (42 attempts), Sept. 5, 1998
492 vs. Vanderbilt (57), Nov. 14, 1998
475 vs. Tennessee (59), Nov. 22, 1997
463 vs. Arkansas (73), Oct. 3, 1998
423 vs. Northeast Louisiana (47), Oct. 18, 1997

Passing
Most Passes Attempted, Career
1,184 (795 comp.), 1996-98

Most Passes Attempted, Season
553 (400 comp.), 1998
547* (363 comp.), 1997
*Led the nation

Most Passes Attempted Game
67 vs. Arkansas (47 comp.), Oct. 3, 1998
66 vs. LSU (41), Nov. 1, 1997
61 vs. Florida (40), Sept. 26, 1998
61 vs. Mississippi State (39), Sept. 6, 1997
59 vs. Florida (33), Sept. 27, 1997

Pass Completions
Most Passes Copmpleted, Career
795 (1,184 att.), 1996-98

Most Passes Completed, Season
400* (553 att.), 1998
363* (547 att.), 1997
*Led the nation

Most Passes Completed, Game
47 vs. Arkansas (67 att.), Oct. 3, 1998
44 vs. Vanderbilt (53), Nov. 14, 1998
41 vs. LSU (66), Nov. 1, 1997
41 vs. Georgia (55), Oct. 25, 1997
40 vs. Florida (61), Sept. 26, 1998

Net Passing Yards
Most Yards Passing, Career
8,435 (795 comp./1184 att.), 1996-98

Most Yards Passing, Season
4,275^ (400 comp./553 att.), 1998
3,884* (363 comp./547 att.), 1997
*Led the nation
^ Ranked second nationally

Most Yards Passing, Game
499 vs. Arkansas (47 comp./67 att.), Oct. 3, 1998
498 vs. Louisville (29 comp./39 att.), Sept. 5, 1998
492 vs. Vanderbilt (44 comp./53 att.), Nov. 14, 1998
476 vs. Tennessee (35 comp./50 att.), Nov. 22, 1997
428 vs. Northeast Louisiana (34 comp./43 att.), Oct. 18, 1997

Completion Percentage
Best Completion Percentage, Career
.671 (795 comp./1184 att.), 1996-98

ADDITIONAL TITLES FROM SPORTS PUBLISHING INC.

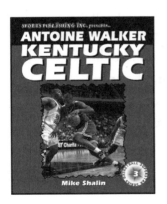